the handmade tile book

liza gardner

photography by emma peios

Trafalgar Square Publishing

To all artists – recognised or not – working in any discipline, in any country.

First published in the United States of America in 1999 by
Trafalgar Square Publishing, North Pomfret, Vermont 05053

Printed and bound in Singapore by Tien Wah Press (Pte) Ltd

ISBN 1-57076-150-7

Library of Congess Catalog Card Number: 98-89997

Editor: Louisa Somerville
Editorial Assistant: Kate Latham
Art Direction: Blackjacks
Photographer: Emma Peios
Managing Editor: Coral Walker

10 9 8 7 6 5 4 3 2 1

Reproduction by Modern Age Repro House Ltd, Hong Kong

Acknowledgements
The author would like to thank John Powell, the helpful librarian at the
Jackfield Tile Museum, Ironbridge, Staffs; Chris Cox, a tile maker at the same location;
Susan Rasey and Roland Letheridge of Marlbourgh Tiles for the kind indulgence shown when
I had the temerity to ask if I could look around their factory; Kate Foster from Fired Earth for the
loan of the tiles shown on pages 6, 7 and 9; Paris Ceramics for the loan of the floor tiles shown
on the front cover and finally, Coral and Kate at New Holland Publishers.

Every effort has been made to present clear and accurate instructions. Therefore, the author and
publishers can offer no guarantee or accept any liability for any injury, illness or damage which
may inadvertently be caused to the user while following these instructions.

contents

introd

Take a walk down main street, through a shopping mall or around an old town. On buildings ancient and modern, from shops, bars and restaurants to churches, public libraries and city halls – everywhere there are tiles! And as you start making your own, you'll notice even more.

Why has this material been used to clad walls, floors and even roofs in such an abundance and for so long? Well, firstly, for decoration. There is endless possibility offered by the wide range of colors, patterns and textures. Secondly, tiles provide a tough and durable finish. Finally, clay – the raw material of tiles – is also widely available throughout the world.

Tile making isn't something that can be achieved in an afternoon. It takes time and patience. However, in most cases you can do a bit, cover your work and return to it later. It is labor-intensive, but the pleasure gained from seeing your work finally fixed in place is immense.

In this book I have tried to illustrate a wide range of techniques used by tile makers. It is not all-encompassing, nor exhaustive. Some methods of manufacture require costly plant, while others involve advanced skill levels, but these things are not essential to make beautiful tiles – as you will see in the 20 glorious designs that follow. There are friezes and panels, number plaques and picture tiles, shaped tiles and terracotta garden pieces. So try your hand by following these designs, or adapt them to suit your location by modifying the colors or details – and you will have the huge satisfaction of creating an environment that is uniquely yours.

uction

tiles
a brief history

Tiles have a long and colorful history and many of those we see today are based on traditional patterns and designs used hundreds or even thousands of years ago.

The basic concept of colored tiles was already in existence in Egypt in 4000 BC. At this time, a crude, turquoise-blue glaze stained with copper was starting to be developed. Soon after this, Egypt was to become the pioneering center for the manufacture of glassware, and with that, came the development of glazes for both architectural and domestic ceramics. By 1180 BC, the Egyptians were scratching pictures and patterns into the clay (called incising) to depict elaborate battle scenes along with representations of flora, fauna, religious symbols and ornamentation. The use of color and motifs had a symbolic significance, as the artists looked to nature and natural forms for the symmetry that is the fundamental precept for all tile design.

Between 1300 and 500 BC, the Assyrians and Babylonians in Mesopotamia developed impressive glazed architectural ceramics. The most famous of these is the Ishtar Gate of Babylon, just south of Baghdad in modern-day Iraq, with its processional passage depicting lions in a glorious red relief against a background of deep turquoise. This created an entrance to the city, honoring the goddess Ishtar and testament to the power and wealth of the patron, Nebuchadnezzar II.

But it was to be many centuries later – in 622 AD – that the founding of the Islamic faith brought forth what was to become the greatest influential source of architectural ceramic design and manufacturing. The earliest Islamic tiles

were made in the ninth century AD. As figurative representation in any form — either human or animal — is forbidden under Islam, artists used hexagons, triangles and simple geometric and naturalistic patterns to decorate tiles for the interiors and exteriors of mosques and palaces.

By the 13th century, strong, bold and intricate patterns were emerging, such as fantastical flowers, blossoms, scrolls and arabesques. These designs were to strongly influence 19th-century English designers, such as William Morris and William de Morgan. Copies of the original tiles are still being commercially produced today – a tribute to the strength and originality of the early designs.

In 16th-century Spain, glazed tiles were being manufactured, an export market to Italy was established, and the Italians soon became inspired makers themselves, developing a method of tin glaze decoration known as majolica. These innovative designs were later to influence the Dutch, Flemish and the English.

Dutch tile manufacturing boomed in the mid-17th century under an expanding and prosperous economy. The emerging middle class was becoming affluent, with money to spend on brick-built houses decorated with tiles. These tiles were tin-glazed and were greatly influenced by Chinese porcelain, not only in color, but also in ornament. Though these tiles were made in many parts of Holland, the name that has now become generic is Delft.

In England this style was embraced when Flemish potters, who had been working in Spain, fled to England to escape persecution during the Spanish Inquisition. The English Delftware industry was to survive for two hundred years in Liverpool, London and Bristol.

Until the 19th century, tile making was a craft-based industry of small workshops. With the advent of the Industrial Revolution in England came new techniques of mass production. The tile industry rapidly expanded, once more becoming fashionable, and medieval, Gothic and Islamic designs were resurrected. However, although the use of tiles was regenerated, it brought about a stagnation in the craft. The tile workshops (known for innovation of design) declined and the industrialists (known for innovation of manufacturing techniques) prospered. Sadly, but almost inevitably, a safe and sterile design period ensued.

The Arts and Crafts Movement attempted to address this situation by setting up small workshops once more to produce tiles. Inspiration, in the main, was taken from John Ruskin's work '*The Stones of Venice*', in which the author expressed a desire to reinvest labor with the pride that comes from a personal input in the process of creating. Fine ideals! All that happened was that once again, only the rich could afford well-designed tiles.

It would appear we shall always live with this situation, the large tile manufacturers only ever innovating in methods of production and cost-cutting, while the products of the smaller firms – who produce some wonderful designs – are outside the price range of most people.

The only way to combat this is to design and make your own tiles!

Left: top right and bottom left are Victorian tiles made by Minton.
The remaining tiles are modern interpretations of traditional designs.
Right: Modern border influenced by 16th-century Isnik designs.

sources of design
and inspiration

I have been a professional ceramist for nearly 20 years, but only began making tiles in any number a few years ago. As an artist, color and shape are important to me and it was because I couldn't find tiles in exactly the hues I wanted, I thought I would make them myself. It was only then that I realized just how easy tile making actually is. Before you begin, consider these aspects:

position and function

When planning to tile an area such as a kitchen, you needn't limit your design to the worktop or splashback – think about edges, ledges, alcoves and shelves, too. Try to create a complete design that will unify the whole. Don't lay relief or heavily textured tiles as a work surface, as they will become a dirt trap; always glaze any edges that will be exposed.

theme and ambience

Think about your chosen pattern or decoration and how it repeats itself. Consider the way in which the design becomes coherent, either by placing a small motif in the corner – as used on the Early English Delft tiles shown – or by using a half or quarter motif which forms a whole when two or four tiles are placed together.

When considering the type of design you want, refer directly to tiles, both historical and contemporary. Look at existing design motifs and symbols of ancient and ethnic cultures. Also, look at more unusual sources such as the print on a dress, an unusual greetings card or your favorite painting or rug. Your library or local bookstore can provide you with source books of designs. These catalogue a range of motifs and patterns.

All of these will provide a rich source for color ideas, but for shapes, think about fittings or details on furniture and architecture, the weave of wicker or willow, even a button on a jacket. This last, in fact, provided the motif for the Turkish Steam Room project on page 72.

Let your imagination run loose. But remember, you'll have to live with your tiles, so trendy motifs or colors that will date in a year or two are best avoided.

color and texture

The palette for modern glazes is almost as extensive as that of manufactured paint, while brush-on glazes have reduced the skill level required for glazing considerably. These are expensive compared to a glaze you mix yourself, but easy to apply and, with the exception of some reds, very consistent. As with most things, larger pots of glaze work out more economical than small ones.

A couple of practical tips to bear in mind: avoid dark colors immediately around sinks, basins and baths as the water splashes will soon mark and look unsightly. Floor tiles should be comfortable to walk on, even in bare feet.

scale

Always work out your design before you start tile making. Begin by plotting the design on to a grid, remembering to allow for grout lines – normally $\frac{1}{8}$ to $\frac{1}{4}$ in (3 to 5 mm) for wall tiles and $\frac{1}{4}$ to $\frac{3}{8}$ in (6 to 9 mm) for floors. This will give you a good impression of the overall effect.

A pattern or color that works on a few tiles could become overpowering when extended over a large area. By using a grid to plan your design you will also be able to forsee any problems that might occur when dealing with awkward shapes, angles or corners.

Don't be too ambitious – a complex design that is satisfying to draw or paint on a test tile, or a section of your grid, could well become an abandoned project when you are halfway through a mammoth installation!

If the design is considered and planned carefully, the tiles well made and installed, they should last as long as the bricks and mortar on to which they've been fitted.

Contemporary versions of early 16th-century English Delft tiles using simple painted boats, houses, flowers and birds.
Small motifs are painted in the corners to connect the 'field' tiles (center left) with the decorated tiles, uniting the design.

tile-making equipment

Ceramics requires a few specialist pieces of equipment, but if you attend a college or are friendly with a potter, you can borrow most of these items and build up your own collection gradually. Most regular, flat tiles can be fired using a tile crank, saving kiln space. However, tiles with raised decoration, or an unusual profile, will need to be fired flat on a kiln shelf.

BATTS: Wooden boards used for drying tiles on.

BANDING WHEEL (NOT SHOWN): Also known as a 'whirler', it is a potter's turntable that comes in various diameters. They are available in cast iron or alloy and are extremely useful for glazing a complete panel when placed on a board. You simply rotate the work, enabling even spray glazing from all directions.

BRUSHES: A range of brushes are necessary for decorating certain tiles. A glaze mop is used for applying brush-on glaze, as it has very soft bristles which eliminate brushstrokes. A fan brush is used for delicate sweeping strokes and a sieve brush is a large, round brush for forcing mixing glaze or slip through a sieve. You'll also need two or three different size artists' paintbrushes when painting on a design.

CHEESE WIRE: This is used to slice off pieces of clay ready for use.

MESH SIEVE: Available in a number of grades and used to sieve powdered glaze to ensure it is lump-free. The number printed on the side of the sieve denotes the amount of holes per square inch, so the higher the number, the finer the mesh.

PLASTIC SCRAPER/METAL KIDNEY (NOT SHOWN): Useful for scraping excess amounts of clay from plaster moulds without scraping away the plaster surface. It also serves to even up the backs of sprigs (see page 17).

POTTER'S OR CLAY CUTTING NEEDLE: Used for cutting around templates to ensure a square edge, they are available in different gauges. Use a heavier gauge that will not bend when you apply pressure.

PRINTING BLOCK: These little wooden blocks were originally used for printing textiles, but they can be picked up quite cheaply from craft or hobby shops and make ideal stamps for picture tiles.

DUST MASK: Necessary safety equipment to prevent you inhaling silica, one of the chief components of clay and glaze.

ROLLING PIN: For rolling out clay to a consistent thickness.

SET SQUARE: Essential for obtaining accurate right angles and a true square for your tiles if you are not using an automatic tile cutter.

SPONGE: For smoothing down wet clay.

STENCIL BRUSH: For stencilling designs on to your tiles.

SURFORM: Useful for cleaning and 'trueing' up the edges of leather-hard tiles and the rough edges of plaster moulds.

TILE CRANK: A stacking system in which to place tiles ready for firing.

TILE CUTTER: A sophisticated, automatic tile cutter which produces the same size tiles quickly and easily off its spring-loaded plate.

TOOTHBRUSH: Use an old one! The ideal tool for 'scoring' a tile ready to receive a sprigged motif.

WIRE MODELLING TOOL: Particularly useful for modelling leather-hard clay and plaster.

making
tiles

The information contained in this section will enable you to embark with some confidence on the creation of unique and original tile projects. The following instructions are purely a starting point, while the Further Reading section will guide you towards some of the more technical books available should you wish to explore ceramics in greater depth (see page 78).

clay

Clay is a messy business, be warned! One of the main components of clay and all glazes is silica, which can be poisonous if inhaled, so remember to keep the dust to a minimum and use a proper dust mask that fully encloses the nose and mouth.

If you want to work on your kitchen table, by all means do, but prior to preparing or consuming any food in the work area, you must thoroughly clean all the surfaces.

A much better solution is to have a dedicated work area, such as a cellar, a shed or garage. If it has a separate entrance from your house, so much the better, as clay footprints over the hall carpet are never really appreciated!

PREPARING CLAY

Raw clay has what is known as a 'memory' of its own. This means that clay will always try to return to the previous shape while being dried out. To reduce the chances of your tiles warping while drying, the following method for forming a slab is recommended.

drying phases of clay

soft *The condition when removed from the polythene bag. Keep handling to a minimum.*

soft leather *Still pliable but will retain a given shape. Depending on the ambient temperature and thickness of the work, clay achieves this state about three hours after being rolled out. Can be handled with care.*

leather-hard *Firm and inflexible but looks and feels damp and cold. Easy to handle and is the perfect stage to decorate, mark or scrape. Ideal time to clean up any damage with a damp sponge and true up uneven edges with a surform.*

bone-dry *Has changed color and become lighter. No longer feels cold. Is very brittle and chips easily. Great care is needed when handling.*

ROLLING OUT: Using a cheese wire, slice a slab of clay from the top of the bag slightly thicker than your planned tiles, (about $\frac{3}{4}$ in [15 mm] thick is needed to create wall tiles finishing at about $\frac{1}{4}$ in [6 mm] and about 1 in [25 mm] for $\frac{3}{8}$ in [9 mm] floor tiles).

Throw the slab on to a piece of heavy canvas or calico. Use some force – really slap it down! This has the benefit of flattening the clay in a natural and unmechanical fashion. Lift it off, turn it over and rotate the slab through 90 degrees and throw it down again.

No matter how hard you manage to hurl the slab down it is inevitable that you will need to roll out the clay as well. Use two thin strips of $\frac{3}{8}$ in (9 mm) wood or ply for wall tiles and a minimum of $\frac{1}{2}$ in (12 mm) for floor tiles. These strips are used as thickness guides and will ensure an even and consistent tile thickness. Use the longest rolling pin you can find, ensuring it is dry, and roll between the wooden strips.

WEDGING

These days, clay is supplied ready-mixed and wrapped in manageable-sized plastic bags. Normally, especially when making flat forms such as tiles, you can use the clay straight from the bag. However, there are times when you will need to do some preparatory work. Two designs in this book use clay that has an added colorant. In these cases – and when you wish to recycle your soft offcuts – you will need to 'wedge' the clay. Wedging is a laborious but necessary process to expel air from the clay and achieve a smooth consistency, returning the clay to its 'fresh from the bag' state. There are many ways to achieve this but the simplest is the 'Bull's Head' method.

Gather up any soft offcuts and roll them into a rough ball. Place the ball in front of you on a wooden batt and

Rolling out: use wooden guides to ensure an even thickness.

Cutting out: a spring-loaded cutter cuts a quick and precise tile.

using the heels of your palms, push down in one vigorous movement into the center and roll the clay forward. Keep your fingers outstretched and lift the clay back towards you after each movement. After about five times the ball will take on the shape of a cylinder with a spiral at each end. Where the heels of the palms are placed, indentations similar to the cheeks of a bull will be formed, with the spirals representing the horns. You can only wedge soft offcuts as any clay that has begun to harden must be fully broken down, dried out, re-wedged and left to mature for six months – a process which is outside the scope of this book.

cutting out

You can cut tiles with a simple pastry cutter when the clay has achieved the soft leather state. A more sophisticated method is to use a tile cutter, which has a spring-loaded plate to make it easier to remove the clay. Use one when your clay is at the more malleable state of soft.

An alternative that gives greater freedom in the shapes you can use, is an accurately measured and cut template of thin card, perspex or plywood. (Don't be too free with the design as the finished tiles have to join in a regular pattern – we're not constructing a mosaic here!)

Remember when planning a design to take note of shrinkage. In earthenware this is about 5 per cent, in terracotta nearer 8 per cent. If you are attempting a fully planned installation involving very few or no cuts at all in the finished tiles, this is obviously very important. (You can 'cheat' the tiles somewhat with the grout lines, but you must keep the width of the lines consistent.)

A large set square, ruler and a compass are useful tools to mark and cut out designs. After removal from the cutting tool or template, lay the raw tiles on to a board to dry out.

drying out

The key to successful, warp-free tiles is to dry them out very, very slowly. The tiles will tend to dry from the corners, causing curling and warping. Slow drying, combined with regular turning and weighting down the tiles will help avoid this problem.

Lay your tiles on a clean, flat, absorbent board (a piece of MDF is ideal). Stack layers of tiles and boards on top of one another, then loosely cover the entire stack with polythene. There are two reasons for stacking the tiles – to save space and to apply pressure.

At least twice a day, rotate the tiles from the center to the edge of each board to ensure even drying, and shuffle the stack, too. Avoid draughts or direct heat.

Tiles that have applied motifs cannot be stacked, so you need to check and rotate them more frequently. If you want to conserve shelf space, use kiln props to raise each subsequent board above the relief on the lower board.

Cutting out: a handmade perspex template serves as a cutting guide for a special tile. The clay is cut with a potter's needle.

decorating tiles

Now the real fun begins. You can decorate tiles in a multitude of ways: with 'sprigged' designs which form a raised motif, by stamping and incising to form indentations, stencilling, sponging or painting a design.

plaster casting and making sprigs

Also known as press-moulding, this simple technique of making a plaster cast from a 'found' object gives your tiles a crisp, 3-D quality, usually only found on more expensive tiles. The decorative motifs are called sprigs.

All of the items I cast are everyday things you can find (hence the term 'found'). Shells picked up from the beach, small architectural motifs from junk shops, wooden or plastic mouldings (large hardware stores are a good hunting ground for these), buttons, kids' toys – in fact, almost anything can be cast.

you will need:
'found' objects, clay, potter's plaster,
potter's needle, petroleum jelly,
wooden board or batt, cardboard,
masking tape

Embedding found objects into a clay slab ready to make a plaster cast (see page 18).

MAKING THE PLASTER CAST Ensure the objects you wish to cast are clean and dust free. On a wooden board, roll out a slab of clay thick enough to hold the objects to be cast.

Lay your objects on the slab. If, when you lay the object on the slab, there are any gaps between it and the clay, press the object down harder into the clay until the gap has disappeared. Now draw around the object with a potter's needle or similar tool, remove the item and gouge out the clay with a modelling tool. Push the item to be cast in the cavity you have just made and smooth the surface of the slab down with your fingers.

Apply a thin layer of petroleum jelly with your fingers to the surface of the objects and the clay slab. This prevents the objects sticking. (Make sure you apply a thin, even coat of petroleum jelly, as any blobs will obscure the detail of your cast and hence the detail of your sprigs.)

Construct a wall of cardboard around the clay slab. This wall should be at least 1 in (2.5 cm) higher than the objects sitting in the slab. Use the tape to bind the walls together and then secure the base of the walls with coils of leftover clay to stop any movement or leakage when the plaster is poured into your cardboard construction.

Fill a jug or bowl with water. Slowly add the powdered plaster by sprinkling it over the surface of the water. When it has absorbed most of the water and can be seen as a peak

breaking through the surface of the water, the plaster can be left to settle for five minutes before being mixed thoroughly. As a guide, use approximately 3 lb (1.5 kg) of potter's plaster to 2 pt (1 liter) of clean water.

Pour the plaster mixture into the cardboard housing, over the objects and dab the final surface with your hands to remove any air bubbles. Lay aside to set. As the plaster begins to set it will become quite warm. This is a normal chemical reaction.

When the plaster has fully set – about an hour or more, depending on the thickness of your mould – remove the walls, turn over the mould and peel away the clay slab. Some objects will be retained by the clay and some by the plaster. Those held by the plaster will have to be carefully removed using a steel modelling tool. Clean up any rough edges of the plaster with a surform. (Dispose of the clay or put it aside to use for further plaster work. It will have become contaminated by the plaster and will be unsuitable for any other work.)

The mould enables you to make as many sprigs as you require. Leave the mould to become bone dry.

APPLYING SPRIGS Once the plaster mould is dry, you can create a sprig by pressing clay into the cavity. Roll out small coils or balls of clay, smooth with your finger to ensure that

Stamping and pressing: the ends of pieces of wood can make interesting stamps for tiles and motifs.

'Key' the area awaiting the sprig with a damp toothbrush.

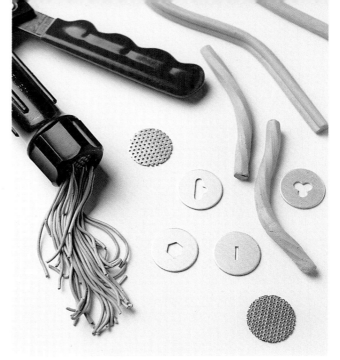

A clay gun and assorted dies. The resulting shapes can be used to create raised patterns and edgings.

there are no creases, and gently press into the mould. Scrape off any excess clay with an old credit card or similar, leaving the surface smooth and level with clean lines on the edge of the sprig. Allow to firm up and then use a small ball of clay to dab the back of the sprig to remove it from the mould.

Place the sprig on the leather-hard tile, draw around it with a potter's needle or pencil and lay it to one side. Using a craft knife, crosshatch the surface of the tile inside the outline of the sprig and dampen the surface with a wet toothbrush. This acts as a 'key' for the sprig. Place the sprig back in position and gently press it down to expel any wet clay, ensuring that there are no gaps. Finally, clean any excess with a damp sponge and, if necessary, clean up the edges with a modelling tool.

STAMPING AND PRESSING A simple method of creating what may seem to be complicated and unusual patterns is by using the ends of different-shaped pieces of wood. This method can encompass printers' blocks, rubber stamps and found objects. A complex pattern can be built up from a simple tool, such as the end of a ballpoint pen. Also, try altering the surface of the clay by pressing or rolling leaves, lace, netting or mesh directly on to the tile.

using a clay gun

A clay gun is a handheld tool that extrudes clay in a similar way to an icing syringe. It comes with different-shaped dies that enable you to make fine and precise coils, half rounds and square sections that are applied to the surface of a tile in the same way as any other sprig. The advantages of a clay gun are speed and the cleanliness of the lines you extrude, but they are a hassle to clean. Remember also that if you make a delicate coil that curls across the tile in a complicated fashion, a correspondingly complicated crosshatch of the tile will be necessary.

modelling

You may wish to create a relief shape so original that you cannot buy or find this shape to take a cast from. Or you might only want to use a motif once, in which case there is no point in making a mould. In either situation, you will need to model the relief from scratch.

Start by drawing the outline on to a board and running a small coil of clay around it to form your design. Build up the relief with small pieces of clay. Use various modelling tools and a craft knife to define any detailing. Work in stages, allowing the clay to dry slightly should the tools stick. Keep adding and removing clay until the desired motif is finished. A damp finger is good for smoothing out any unwanted blemishes.

decorating slip

Slip is clay in a liquid state. Its prime function is to change the surface color of your tile by brushing on or dipping. Slip can also be used for a technique called inlaying (see page 69) but only for fine lines or very small areas.

You can prepare your own slip and color it with oxides or body stains but it is also available ready-mixed in a wide choice of colors.

To make slip you will need bone-dry clay, crushed in a polythene bag to contain the dust. Carefully transfer it into a plastic bowl. If a pigment is to be added to the clay, the colorant and clay should be weighed and the pigment added at this stage.

for white slip:
1 lb (500 g) of dry white earthenware should be dissolved in 2 pt (1 liter) of clean water.

for terracotta slip:
To 1 lb (500 g) of dry white earthenware add 3 oz (75 g) of red iron oxide and dissolve in 2 pt (1 liter) of water.

Set aside for at least six hours or until the clay has completely broken down. The water will have separated and it will need to be mixed well. Pour the mix through a 30-mesh sieve. (A nylon washing-up brush is excellent for forcing the slip through the mesh.) The slip should be the consistency of thick custard. If it is too thin, leave it to dry out; add more water if it is too thick.

Slip should be applied at soft leather or leather-hard stage, if applied by brush. If dipping tiles, only apply at leather-hard. Never attempt to apply slip to a bone-dry tile – it will crack and fall off.

To brush the slip on, load a small mop brush and apply with bold strokes across the tile, starting at the top and working your way down. Set aside to dry off and apply further coats if streaky. This method is best used for small areas or details.

A far quicker method of applying slip is to dip the face of your tile into the mix. This method has the disadvantage of making the dipped tile softer and more difficult to handle. Hold the tile at the edges with your thumb and forefinger and dip it into the slip at a slight angle with a slow swooping motion. Lift it out and carefully set it aside until it reverts back to leather-hard. If you find the slip surface uneven, carefully level off using the edge of a steel kidney in a scraping motion.

underglaze colors

Underglaze colors are painted or sponged on 'under the glaze' at either leather-hard or bone-dry stage. Underglazes come in a wide range of colors and are available as powder, ready-mixed tubes or tubs.

Powder and tubes can be applied as a wash, like water colors, whereas the tub form tends to have the flat properties of gouache. Apply them with a loaded brush to give a good coat of color. Mix the powder form with water or a water-based medium. The medium acts as a binder to help adhesion and prevent smudging.

Underglazes can be applied in any way you might apply emulsion paint, such as by using a brush, sponge, roller, stencil or stamp.

Two white tiles that have been dipped into terracotta slip. Any ridges or blemishes can be smoothed out with a steel kidney when the tiles are leather-hard.

The left-hand tile has been dipped in blue alkaline glaze, while the right-hand tile awaits the pleasure.

glazing and firing

mixing & applying glaze

When you coat a tile with glaze you provide a waterproof barrier to the surface. As glaze is made from powdered glass, always wear a dust mask when mixing or spraying it. Always spray glaze in a special booth fitted with an extractor.

Glaze is available as a ready-mixed powder called 'slop', or in 'brush-on' form. Slop is normally only available from large suppliers or direct from the glaze manufacturers. Brush-on glaze is far more expensive, but contains additives

which prevent the glaze appearing streaky and eliminate brush marks when fired.

There are many different glaze types and numerous glaze recipe books, which can guide you to achieve almost any color or texture that you wish. As you gain more experience using glazes, you will be able to develop your own shades and textures.

Throughout this book I have used a range of earthenware glazes. These glazes form a layer on the top of the clay surface that is relatively soft, but give excellent color responses. In contrast, stoneware or porcelain glazes are extremely tough and actually permeate the surface of the

clay when fired. Earthenware glazes are generally available in three different firing ranges, the higher the temperature the harder the surface.

low temperature	1562-1868°F (850–1020°C)
mid temperature	1832-2084°F (1000–1140°C)
high temperature	2012-2156°F (1100–1180°C)

Commercial glazes are more stable and reliable but can be limiting; there are times when a specific color or texture can only be achieved by following a recipe, such as with the dry barium glaze used on the Terracotta Garden Panel on

color variables

all glazes use a base component that affects the color response.

Lead-based glazes give a slightly yellow tone and, by the addition of copper carbonate between 1-3 per cent, a range of leaf greens is obtained. Adding 1-5 per cent iron oxide will result in a rich palette of honey and ochre shades. The addition of cobalt will result in a greeny-blue shade, the amounts to add would be between 0.5-2 per cent.

Unlike lead, the color responses to borax and alkaline are quite different. Borax is in fact an alkaline glaze, albeit with a low alkaline content, and it is this base glaze that I tend to use for my lead-free transparent glaze. The overall tone is much colder than lead with a slight blue hue, the copper added in the proportions mentioned above will give a bluer tone with the borax, becoming turquoise with the alkaline. The blues obtained from the addition of cobalt will become more vibrant and deeper in tone in both borax and alkaline. I do not recommend the addition of iron oxide to these two glazes as the result is invariably a rather unattractive greeny-brown color.

If you are following a recipe or buying your glaze in powdered form you will have to add water and weigh the components out. Should you wish to add color to a clear glaze powder or alter the color of a manufacturer's colored powder glaze, add your colorant to the glaze prior to the water. A word of caution – if you use any lead-based glazes with copper carbonate or copper oxide as the colorant on your tiles, never prepare food directly on to them.

page 31 and the rich alkaline glaze on the Rococo Relief tiles on page 56.

The glaze I usually use is a clear, lead-free, mid-temperature glaze with a firing range of between 1920–1980°F (1050–1080°C). The reason for using a clear glaze is that any detailing can be seen through the glazed surface, as if through glass. This coating of glaze can be either clear or opaque depending on the colorant added.

Having added the colorant and water, mix together. Sieve the resulting mixture through a 120-mesh sieve into a spotlessly clean lidded bowl or bucket. This will be your stock glaze and you should decant it as required into the final applicator, ie. a paint tray for dipping or a spray gun for spraying. If you are spraying the glaze, you will need to achieve the consistency of single cream. For dipping your tiles, a thinner mix (about 25 per cent thinner) will be needed. This is because the dipped tile absorbs more water from the glaze mix.

Dipping is by far the best method for tiles. Use your thumb and forefinger to hold the tile (as for coating with slip) but dip the tile face down into the glaze. Hold the tile in place for a few seconds, avoiding spills on the edges and back, and lift out. Touch up any missed areas with a brush. Leave to dry and wipe the back of the tile clean with a damp sponge.

If you spray your glaze, be careful not to apply it too thickly as this will make it crawl, craze or pool on the face of the tile when fired. The main advantage of spraying is that it allows a graduation of color.

For brushing-on you must use a pre-mixed glaze. Follow the manufacturer's instructions for this method.

firing

Should you purchase a kiln, there are some reasonably priced electric kilns available. The smaller models can be placed on a worktop and plugged straight into an ordinary wall socket. These electric kilns are simple to use and the addition of a controller, either electronic or mechanical will further aid your firing process.

Most work entails two firings. The first, called a **BISQUE OR BISCUIT FIRING**, is done when the tile is absolutely bone dry. Usually fire to about 1830°F (1000°C).

The secondary firing is called a **GLAZE OR GLOST FIRING**, the object being to melt the glaze and fuse it to the body of

Alkaline glazed tiles in a crank, fresh from the kiln.

the tile. The final temperature will vary according to the type of glaze used, but can be as high as 2372°F (1300°C).

A third firing is for decorative applications added to a glazed surface, such as transfers, onglaze painting or lusters. This firing is much lower – between 1380–1470°F (750–800°C). Ventilate the space well when firing lusters as the fumes can be noxious.

A concern of great importance when firing any stage is the rate of 'ramp'. This is the amount you increase the temperature in the early stages of a firing to expel water or gasses, usually referred to as 'a ramp of 'x' degrees per hour'. Refer to the kiln manufacturer's manual.

Allow the kiln to cool naturally, do not attempt to speed up the process of cooling by opening the lid prematurely as this will result in your tiles splitting or cracking.

packing a kiln

To maximise space in the kiln, tiles are usually packed in tile cranks. Each crank holds about 30 tiles. Large tiles, such as floor tiles or tiles with a raised decoration, have to be laid singly on a kiln shelf.

In a bisque firing you can stack tiles one on top of another, but make sure the stack is regular to avoid the danger of warping if one tile overhangs the one below. 4 in (100 mm) square and 6 in (150 mm) square tiles can be stacked three or four tiles high in the kiln. Larger tiles, 8 in (200 mm) in any direction should only be stacked two high. Any larger tiles, say 12 in (300 mm) and above, need to be placed on the shelf singly.

Cranks are really efficient for glaze firings – although irregular tiles and those with a raised relief can only be fired on a shelf. Do not allow any edges of tiles either loose-laid or in cranks to touch, as the glaze will melt each tile together.

fixing tiles

When fixing tiles to a surface that is subject to any type of movement, such as wooden worktops or table tops, you must use a tile cement that flexes slightly. Likewise, when fixing exterior installations, be sure to use the correct adhesive and grout.

Normally this information can be gleaned from a DIY book or a fact sheet provided by most tile manufacturers. These booklets will tell you how to set out a tiling installation, the tools required and exactly what materials to use. You may have to make adjustments to the normal recommendations according to the results of your tiles.

To space your handmade tiles, sort the tiles by size. Lay each row with tiles of a similar size. If there is a variation in thickness of your tiles, start by laying the thickest tiles and compensate on the thinner ones by using a thicker layer of tile cement. You can also do this to overcome the problem of warping.

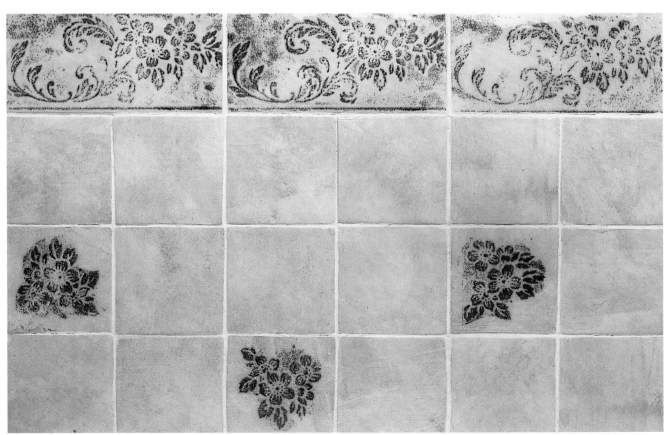

Variation in tile size can be 'cheated' by adjusting the grout lines.

tiles to

The following designs are also a library of techniques with a variety of color choices so that you may experiment, if you wish. You can use them as a springboard for your own ideas, to infuse any given theme with your personal design.

Take care to measure your site accurately, taking into account the width of the grout lines and also the shrinkage of the clay whilst drying. If the tiles are too large, cutting them is a solution, albeit time-consuming and tedious, but errors leading to installations that are too small will prove to be far more difficult to correct. A scale drawing, or even a full-size drawing for complicated installations, will help you achieve the accuracy of design that sets apart the carefully considered installation from that which is merely cobbled together.

You will need access to a kiln for the majority of the designs, except the House Number Plaque on page 62, Sari Sari on page 64 and the Gilded Quarry Tiles on page 59. This last technique is probably the one with the most potential for you to infuse with your own ideas as it enables you to use acrylics, poster colors or even household emulsion paint for a floor tile scheme.

With some practice and not a little patience, making your own tiles will become highly rewarding. The sense of achieving a splash of interior decoration that is truly unique, eye-catching and practical is fabulous, and who knows, a friend or a neighbor may be so impressed that they will want some tiles made as well. Perhaps this could lead to the start of a fulfilling new business venture.

make

SPRIGGING

One way of altering the surface of a tile is by sprigging. This involves adding a raised relief on to a flat tile to make it three-dimensional. One of the best known examples of sprigging is the work of Joshia Wedgwood who – in conjunction with the modelling skills of the sculptors John Flaxman (both senior and junior) – refined the technique in a hugely successful emulation of ancient Greek ceramic art. The ceramic invention that will always be associated with Wedgwood is the superb Jasper ware – a high-fired stoneware body of pale blue with white sprigs depicting classical motifs placed on splendid forms.

These tile motifs are based on oak, sycamore and maple leaves, stained in autumnal colors, but there is no reason why you couldn't buy pre-colored clays or stain your clay any color you wish. When choosing the size of the motifs, bear in mind the eventual location. Most wall tiles are 4 or 6 in (100 or 150 mm) square.

leaf motifs

To make your own sprigs you will need to master the simple technique of plaster casting (see page 17). To take full advantage of any detailing in the reliefs you create – and the more detail the better – use a clear transparent glaze.

The idea for these little motifs as 'stick-ons' came to me several years ago. As the main body of my work has always used sprigging on bowls and vases, I have always ended up with far more sprigs than I could use. How could all these excess sprigs be utilized? The idea of sticking them on to existing tiles in a bathroom, kitchen or shower room – thus giving the wall a quick makeover – proved to be a very successful one, and I have made many sprigged motifs since.

skills required
- ❏ plaster casting and making sprigs, page 17-18
- ❏ wedging, page 12
- ❏ drying out, page 15
- ❏ bisque firing, page 24

equipment:
batts, pencil, small board, tracing paper,
8 oz (250 g) smooth modelling clay,
modelling tools, plaster, strong plastic bag,
craft or potter's knife, potter's needle,
bowl, water, sponge, rubber gloves,
rolling pin, plastic scraper or old credit card

clay and body stains:
To make about 20 motifs you will need
1 lb (500 g) dry white earthenware clay with either:
2 oz (50 g) rutile (dark beige-brown)
or
$\frac{1}{2}$ oz (10 g) copper carbonate (dark green)
or
$\frac{3}{4}$ oz (20 g) red iron oxide (terracotta)
or
$\frac{1}{2}$ oz (10 g) chromium oxide (sage green)

Firstly, the mould for the leaf motif must be made. Draw an outline of a leaf on to a board, roll out a small coil of clay to lay along this outline and build up the basic shape of the leaf using little pieces of clay. Smooth with your fingers or tools as you go. Leave to dry a little, refine the detailing and put aside to dry to leather-hard.

Refine the detailing further by carving or cutting. Use a damp sponge to clean up any unwanted marks or hard edges. You are now ready to take a plaster cast and to make your mould.

While your mould is drying, you can prepare the clays. Weigh out the dry clay and colored pigments and place into the plastic bag and secure. Gently crush the mixture with the rolling pin to break the clay into small pieces. Shake the bag to mix the clay and pigments together. Carefully pour into a bowl, cover the mixture with water and leave to stand for at least six hours so that the clay can break down completely.

Once dissolved, let the mixture dry out quickly to a manageable consistency. This process can be speeded up by putting it on to a plaster batt or other absorbent surface. Do not allow it to dry out too much. Wedge thoroughly to get rid of lumps and continue to wedge until the clay feels plastic and smooth but not sticky. Bag it up until ready to use.

Fill the mould with clay and let it firm up. Remove from the mould, place on the batt and allow to dry. Then bisque fire to 2050°F (1120°C).

terracotta garden panel

This is a more ambitious project because of the intricacy of the sprigging and the large section of curved framing. The motifs are Tudor-style roses mixed with classic architectural forms, which you will have to model. This is not hard, it just takes a little practice and perseverance. The design uses a number of different sprigs which, of course, you can adapt. Some of the detail is taken from junk items – just use your imagination when choosing alternatives! This panel would look good mounted on a garden wall, either ancient or modern.

skills required
❏ rolling out, page 12
❏ cutting out, page 14
❏ plaster casting and making sprigs, page 17
❏ modelling, page 19
❏ drying out, page 15
❏ mixing and applying glaze, page 22
❏ bisque and glaze firing, page 24

equipment:
batts, pencil, tracing paper, craft knife or potter's knife, 4 in (100 mm) square tile cutter or template, 4 x 8 in (100 x 200 mm) template, modelling tools, clay gun, potter's needle, $8\frac{1}{4}$ in (210 mm) architrave mold, acanthus, border and button molds, bowl, water, sponge, plant mist spray, rubber gloves, plaster, rolling pin, rolling guides, calico, plastic scraper or old credit card, small mop brush, fine paintbrush (no. 8), toothbrush

clay:
to make 27 tiles 4 x 4 in (100 x 100 mm) and one tile 4 x 8 in (100 x 200 mm) you will need 30 lb (15 kg) red earthenware (terracotta) clay

to make the blue glaze:
10 oz (275 g) nepheline syenite
6 oz (160 g) barium carbonate
$1\frac{1}{2}$ oz (35 g) china clay
$\frac{3}{4}$ oz (20 g) copper carbonate
$\frac{1}{2}$ oz (10 g) lithium
(Lithium is even more toxic than most glaze materials, so wear gloves and a dust mask.)

Dissolve all the ingredients in about 1 pt (500 ml) of water and sieve. Now the glaze is ready to be brushed on.

you will also need:
2 fl oz (60 ml) dark green brush-on glaze
2 fl oz (60 ml) white ready-mixed underglaze

prepare the following sprigs and wrap in polythene to keep damp:
modelled Tudor roses 1 x $3\frac{1}{8}$ in (80 mm) diameter, 2 x 2 in (50 mm) diameter, 5 x $1\frac{1}{4}$ in (30 mm) diameter
12 modelled vine leaves in various sizes
architrave sprigs $8\frac{1}{4}$ x $\frac{3}{4}$ in (210 x 17 mm) for the border and scrolls
4 acanthus sprigs for the bottom of the panel
acanthus sprigs (taken from wooden moulding) for the finial
border sprigs for the base of the vase
21 button sprigs for the body of the vase
half-round extrusions approximately $1\frac{3}{4}$ x 1 in (45 x 25 mm) for the vase, stalks and vines

BASIC TILES Prepare and cut your tiles and leave to dry leather-hard. Lay the tiles together on a large batt with 5 tiles along the width and 6 tiles along the length. Place the 4 x 8 in (100 x 200 mm) tile vertically in the center of the top row. Draw your design on a grid and transfer it to the tiles. Score all lines where a sprig will be placed, using the main photograph as your guide.

BORDER Dampen the architrave sprigs with the mist spray and place around the edge of the tiles to create the border.

This panel emulates a carved bas-relief, with motifs chosen to reinforce this effect. The design is, to some degree, based on 16th-century brick facings, so dry blue barium glaze has been selected to give it an ancient, weathered look, similar to verdigris.

Make six scrolls for the corners and the shoulders of the panel, three curving to the left and three curving to the right. Lay a length of the moulding on a board. Cut to a point about $\frac{1}{4}$ in (5 mm) long and hold it with your left hand about $\frac{1}{4}$ in (5 mm) from the shoulder of the point. With your right hand, ease the point around to start forming a spiral, either to the left or right, as shown below. Slowly and gently ease the point into a spiral with your right thumb and with your left hand ease the architrave around. If you feel any resistance or tension that might cause cracking, dampen it a little more. Continue easing around until you have formed a spiral, as shown. If necessary, remodel any detail that may have been damaged.

Place the scrolls in position and cut to the right size. Position the adjoining architrave with about 1 in (20 mm) overlaying the scroll and scribe a curve to match the edge of the scroll. The architrave should butt cleanly up to the scroll. Continue with all the other scrolls before fixing in place. Cut a miter on the center top tile (see page 36). When all the border pieces are cut and in the correct positions, they can be fixed into place. Start with the bottom left-hand scroll and work your way around in a clockwise direction. Lift each piece aside and dampen the score marks with a wet toothbrush, replace the piece and press into place. Pay extra attention to the joins on the scrolls and the miter at the top. Smooth the joins with a damp finger or modelling tool to conceal them and remove any excess slurry with a damp sponge.

Use a craft knife to cut the tiles carefully to shape around the finial and the scrolls, then smooth the join between the moulding of the border and tiles with a modelling tool.

VASE Lay a length of the extruded beading to outline the vase shape. Cut it to fit, dampen the tile and press the beading in place. Continue by making the handles in the same way. Position the sprigs – taken from a moulding – at the base of the vase, cut to shape and fix down. Fix the button sprigs on the body of the vase.

ROSES Position and fix the Tudor roses, starting with the $\frac{3}{8}$ in (8 mm) rose in the center of the tile below the finial. Lay out extruded lengths of beading and bend into position to form the stems. Work on one stem at a time, dampen the surface and press it in place. When all are firmly positioned, separate each tile with a craft knife. Should the end lift slightly, dampen the underside and re-secure.

OTHER DECORATIONS Place the four acanthus sprigs at the bottom of the panel on either side of the vase, dampen and fix. Position the acanthus taken from the wooden detail at the top of the finial. Dampen the architrave well and carefully ease the acanthus round following the form of the architrave to ensure a snug fit.

Now fit the vines and leaves. Starting from the base of the panel, lay a length of beading and, following the scored marks, ease it over the borders and back on to the main body of the panel. This may have to be done with two or three lengths. Retouch it to disguise the joins. Lay the vine leaves in place, dampen and fix. Take care, when laying over the moulding, that the leaves are fully secure.

GLAZING Highlight small areas of the leaves and stems using white underglaze applied with a small brush. These areas will be glazed later and the white will lift the colors. Leave to dry very slowly. Bisque fire to 1830°F (1000°C). Because of the thickness of these tiles you will have to lay them flat on the kiln shelves, instead of using a tile crank.

Remove from the kiln and brush off any dust. Prepare the blue glaze. Lay out the tiles in the correct order on a board. Load a small mop brush and apply the blue glaze to the body of the vase. Use a small brush to glaze the acanthus leaves and roses. Clean any errors with a craft knife and finish with a damp sponge. Use a small brush to paint the vines and leaves with the dark green glaze. Leave to dry and clean up any glaze spills from the edges of the tiles. Glaze fire to 1920–1960°F (1050–1070°C).

neptune borders

Use these ocean-inspired tiles with subtle blends of green, blue and splashes of ochre to create the ripple effect of moving water. You can use them as a border for plain tiles to create a decorative panel, place them as a dado running around a room or frame your washstand or bath with them. Owing to the marine theme, I would opt to place these tiles in a bathroom. However, when I finally get my swimming pool built, I'll definitely have it tiled like this!

skills required
- ❑ rolling out, page 12
- ❑ cutting out, page 14
- ❑ drying out, page 15
- ❑ plaster casting and making sprigs, pages 17-18
- ❑ bisque firing, page 24
- ❑ mixing and applying glaze, page 22
- ❑ glaze firing, page 24

equipment:
batts, rolling pin, guides, calico, ruler,
pencil or ballpoint pen, 4 in (100 mm) square template,
4 x 8 in (100 x 200 mm) template, craft knife,
potter's needle, toothbrush, bowl, water, sponge,
plastic scraper or old credit card, surform,
small fan paintbrush, dust mask (essential),
spray gun and compressed air

prepare the following plaster casts:
two decorative scrolls about $2\frac{1}{2}$ x 1 in (60 x 25 mm),
    one left-handed and one right-handed
shell about 2 in (50 mm) in diameter
length of wooden architrave $8\frac{1}{4}$ x $\frac{1}{2}$ in (210 x 12 mm)

clay:
to make a panel 24 x 16 in (600 x 400 mm) comprising four
    corner tiles, six border tiles and eight field tiles you will
    need 20 lb (10 kg) white earthenware clay

to make the blue glaze:
2 lb (1 kg) lead-free earthenware transparent glaze
1 oz (20 g) cobalt carbonate

to make the green glaze:
1 lb (500 g) lead-free earthenware transparent glaze
$\frac{1}{2}$ oz (15 g) copper carbonate

to make the ochre glaze:
1 lb (500 g) lead-free earthenware transparent glaze
$\frac{1}{4}$ oz (5 g) rutile
$\frac{1}{4}$ oz (5 g) vanadium pentoxide

BASIC TILES Prepare and cut out the following tiles: six at 4 x 8 in (100 x 200 mm), four at 4 in (100 mm) square and eight at $3\frac{3}{4}$ in (97 mm) square. Leave to dry leather-hard. True the edges and sponge clean. (The eight field tiles are slightly smaller to accommodate the extra grout line needed when fitting as a panel.)

Lay the tiles on a batt into a rectangle with the 4 in (100 mm) tiles in each corner. The 4 x 8 in (100 x 200 mm) tiles are ranged around the edges, one on each side and two at top and bottom. The smaller $3\frac{3}{4}$ in (97 mm) tiles are placed in the center. Cover the assembly with polythene while you prepare your sprigs.

BORDER Roll out a coil of clay and press into a mould for the architrave, scraping off any excess. Remove from the mould. Make all the moulding you will need, cut to the exact size and keep it damp.

Mark out the width of architrave on to the tiles all the way around the edge. Score the surface and dampen all the borders except the corners with a wet toothbrush. Starting with the rectangular tiles, position the moulding in place using gentle pressure. Wipe off any excess with a damp sponge.

MITRING For the corner, you will need to cut a miter at the intersection. Cut two lengths of architrave to fit, position the side moulding first and place the horizontal moulding on top as shown below. With a ruler placed diagonally across the tile, mark and cut the diagonal from the horizontal. This will leave you with a small triangle to discard.

Keeping the horizontal still in position, use the cut diagonal as a guide and cut the side moulding. Score and dampen the tile and press the mouldings in place. Butt the miters together firmly, taking care not to distort them. Gently smooth over the miter to conceal the join with a damp finger. Repeat this process on the remaining corner tiles.

SPRIGGING To decorate the corners, fill and remove 10 shell sprigs from a shell mould and put six under wraps. Place the remaining four shells on to each of the corners and draw around them with the potter's knife. Score and dampen the tiles with a toothbrush and position the shells.

Mark out the center of the rectangular tiles and position the remaining shells. Score the surface, dampen and apply the shells. Fill the scroll mould. (You will need six left and six right-handed motifs.) Fix the scrolls symmetrically to the left and right of the shells.

DRYING OUT No matter how slowly and carefully you dry out a sprigged tile, there is always a risk that the sprigs will start to lift. This is because larger sprigs will cause the tile to dry unevenly. They will need checking almost on a two-hourly basis throughout the day for the first couple of days. If this problem arises, gently ease the sprig back into place. A fine spray of water applied to the back of the sprig should help. Repair any damage by smoothing down with a modelling tool. Should the tiles start to curl from the corners, again gently ease them down. At the end of each working day, loosely cover the tiles with polythene until they eventually reach a bone-dry state. The time this process takes is difficult to estimate depending on the ambient temperature and humidity of your workshop but in a temperate climate, a week is about normal.

FIRING When you have ensured that the tiles are fully dry, bisque fire to 1830°F (1000°C).

When cold, remove the tiles from the kiln and ensure that they are dust-free. Pay extra attention to the areas around the shells and scrolls to prevent the danger of glaze crawling. Assemble the panel on a batt, leaving a space of about $\frac{1}{8}$ in (2 mm) between each tile.

GLAZING Spray the blue glaze evenly on to the panel, remembering to glaze the external edges of the borders well, allow to dry. Clean the spray gun and apply the green glaze in patches to vary the final color tones. Using a small fan brush dipped and generously loaded with the ochre glaze, splash at random across the panel. This will create a dappled effect when the glazes melt. Allow the glaze to dry, then carefully clean off any excess glaze from the backs and inside edges of the tiles with a damp sponge. Fire to 1940-1980°F (1060-1080°C).

Mitring the corners of the border: here, you can see clearly how the clay border is overlapped then cut to create a professional finish.

edwardian checkerboard

A simple, yet attractive, way to relieve the clinical quality of white tiles is to insert alternating terracotta tiles. In fact all the tiles are made from terracotta clay, but the white ones are dipped into slip once they have been cut and dried to leather-hard. The little round motifs can be cast from any 'found' object of a suitable size and shape.

skills required
- ❏ plaster casting and making sprigs, page 17-18
- ❏ using a clay gun, page 19
- ❏ decorating slip, page 20
- ❏ bisque and glaze firing, page 24
- ❏ mixing and applying glaze, page 22

equipment:
batts, pencil, motifs for plaster casting (large and small), toothbrush, craft knife, potter's needle, bowl, water, sponge, rubber gloves, plaster, rolling pin, strong plastic bag, plastic scraper or old credit card, 4 in (100 mm) tile cutter or template, clay gun, steel ruler, fan brush

clay and glaze:
to make about 20 tiles you will need 20 lb (10 kg) smooth terracotta clay, 2 lb (1 kg) transparent lead-free glaze, 1 lb (500 g) white decorating slip, 2 lb (1 kg) white earthenware glaze

SPRIGS Make your moulds for the sprigs. The reliefs on the tiles are taken from a chandelier crystal.

TILES Prepare and cut out the basic tiles to 4 in (100 mm) square and leave until soft leather.

Work out how many border tiles you will need. Mark and cut the required number of tiles in half. Leave all the tiles to dry till leather-hard.

Divide the square tiles into two piles, cover half plus the border tiles with polythene. Dip the remaining tiles in white slip. Leave until leather-hard, then clean and true. Leave to dry. Remove the remaining tiles from the polythene, clean and true, ready to decorate.

DECORATION Mark and score the surfaces of the second batch of tiles ready for the sprigs. Using plaster moulds, press out the sprigs and dampen each tile. Position and press the sprigs in place. Clean up and allow to dry very slowly. With a pencil, mark out and score the positions of the edging and the small roundels on the border tiles. Sprig the small roundels in place.

With a half-round die in the clay gun, extrude strips of beading and place top and bottom of the border tiles. Brush with white slip. Leave till leather-hard, clean, allow to dry. Bisque fire to 2048°F (1120°C). Remove from kiln, brush off dust.

GLAZING Dip the plain white tiles and borders in white glaze and leave to dry. Dip the terracotta decorated tiles in transparent glaze and allow to dry. Wipe the backs. Fire all tiles to 1940–1980°F (1060–1080°C).

INCISING & SGRAFFITO

these techniques have been grouped together as they both involve carving or scratching into the surface of a leather-hard tile. A method of drawing with a ball-point pen or a blunt pencil on to a tile is known as incising. This is not to be confused with sgraffito, a similar method which entails scratching a design on the top surface to reveal another color of clay under the scored or incised line.

Because you are working with only one type of clay, incising has none of the technical difficulties inherent in sgraffito and is therefore recommended for the novice.

The difficulty in undertaking sgraffito is trying to match the shrinkage rates of the various clays.

To illustrate this, look at page 25 which explains the necessity of using a flexible tile cement when bonding tiles to a wooden surface. In the same way that wood and ceramic tiles expand and contract at differing rates, different clays are also subject to this phenomenon. Careful drying out of your tiles will minimise this risk.

With sgraffito, a slip can be brushed on to either a leather-hard or a bisque tile. A gradual layering of the secondary clay will help obtain a suitable match. A useful way around this problem is to use underglazes to achieve the color of the overlay. More of this later on page 45.

piscean panel

I have been adapting and changing this successful design for years. Because of the way the fish chase each other's tails, it is a pattern that lends itself to any circular shape. The design is incised.

The diameter of the central disc is not important and will, no doubt, be governed by your choice of site. The four segments around the fish panel should be in proportion to the disc.

Another point to consider is that if this panel is to be used in conjunction with other tiles, the overall dimensions should be a multiple of the surrounding tiles, e.g. if the tiles are 6 in (150 mm) square with a grout line of $\frac{1}{8}$ in (3 mm) your finished size panel should be 30 in (762 mm) square, that is five tiles wide, five high with four grout spaces between. Remember also to allow for 5 per cent shrinkage when the clay dries.

skills required
- [ ] rolling out, page 12
- [ ] cutting out, page 14
- [ ] drying out, page 15
- [ ] mixing and applying glaze, page 22
- [ ] bisque and glaze firing, page 24

equipment:
rolling pin, guides, calico, batts, ruler, set square, pencil or ballpoint pen, tracing paper, craft knife, potter's needle, bowl, water, sponge, small paintbrush, dust mask (essential), banding wheel, spray gun and compressed air

clay:
to make the tiles you will need 20 lb (10 kg) white earthenware clay and 1 oz (25 g) rutile

to make the blue glaze:
2 lb (1 kg) lead-free earthenware transparent glaze
$\frac{3}{4}$ oz (20 g) cobalt carbonate

This piece could be mounted either as an interior wall panel or outside as part of a water feature.
The subtle gradation of blues and greens, in keeping with the watery theme, was achieved by spray glazing.

to make the green glaze:

2 lb (1 kg) lead-free earthenware transparent glaze

$1\frac{1}{4}$ oz (30 g) copper carbonate

BASIC PANEL On a batt covered with a calico cloth, roll out a slab of clay about $\frac{3}{8}$ in (9 mm) thick and about 18 in (450 mm) square. Lay your design over the slab and transfer on to the damp clay. Allow it to firm up for an hour or so, then using a set square and a potter's needle, cut off the excess. Use a potter's needle or craft knife to cut out each individual tile. Lay aside to dry until leather-hard.

Using a blunt pencil, draw the shapes of the fish and the scales on the central disc plus the scrolls and scallops on the border tiles. Keep an even pressure and try to draw freely. Brush away any loose or raised clay. Smooth down the edges of the cuts with a damp sponge. Use a small paint

Use a set square and potter's needle to cut out the complete panel – you will divide it into tiles later.

brush to color the fins, tail and eyes of the fish with rutile. You can also paint the four corner shells. Allow to dry and then bisque fire to 2048°F (1120°C).

GLAZING When cold, remove the tiles from the kiln and ensure that the surfaces are dust free. Assemble the panel on a batt, leaving a space of about $\frac{1}{8}$ in (2 mm) between each tile. Place the batt and tiles on a banding wheel. (This is not essential, but will aid your control when spraying.)

Before applying the glaze, practise using the spray gun on scrap paper with colored water until you have sufficient control of the gun so that an even layer of glaze will be deposited on the tiles. Use even strokes without stopping or pausing, especially at the end of a stroke.

Glaze the body of the fish and the scrolled border tiles using the transparent glaze with added cobalt. Clean your spray gun, then apply the copper glaze. You could add some food coloring in the glaze to make it easier to see the two different colors. Allow the glaze to dry, then carefully clean off any excess glaze from the backs of the tiles with a damp sponge. Fire to 1940-1980°F (1060-1080°C).

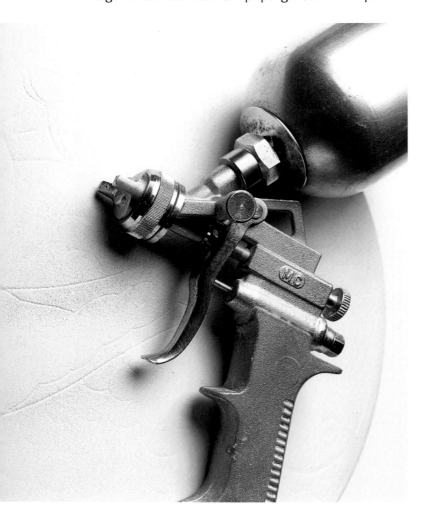

If you are unfamiliar with spray glazing, practise first to ensure success on an ambitious panel such as this.

fossilized leaves

I call these fossilized leaves because they have two levels, like the strata of rock. When you peel off the leaf from a decorated tile, the contrasting clay underneath is revealed. Tiles such as these look best sited outside. If you have a location in mind, do a simple sketch which will give an idea of how many tiles you need, and how many of these need to be white or terracotta. Also consider how many will have leaf decoration. If a symmetrical arrangement is required, remember to specify the direction that the leaves should flow.

skills required
- [ ] rolling out, page 12
- [ ] cutting out, page 14
- [ ] decorating slip, page 20
- [ ] drying out, page 15
- [ ] mixing and applying glaze, page 22
- [ ] bisque and glaze firing, page 24

equipment:
rolling pin, guides, calico, batts,
4 in (100 mm) template or tile cutter,
craft knife, potter's needle, steel palette,
fan brush, bowl, water, sponge, paint tray, surform,
selection of fresh leaves in good condition

clay:
to make about 50 tiles, each 4 in (100 mm) square, you will
    need 40 lb (20 kg) white earthenware clay, 1 pt
    (500 ml) white slip, 1 pt (500 ml) terracotta slip

to make the clear glaze:
4 lb (2 kg) lead-free earthenware transparent glaze

to make the amber glaze:
4 lb (2 kg) lead-free earthenware transparent glaze
$1\frac{3}{4}$ oz (40 g) red iron oxide

Prepare and cut out your tiles, then leave them to stand until soft leather. Now cover half the tiles loosely with polythene. Apply a coat of thick, chocolatey terracotta slip to the remainder with a glaze mop. Leave to dry to soft leather. You need only decorate about a third of the tiles – the rest

will remain plain. Select an even number of both colors and, working on one tile at a time, lay a leaf on to the tile and gently press into the clay (page 41). Take care not to damage the edges of your tile. Set aside and leave to dry leather-hard.

All the decorated tiles will now be dipped in the opposite color slip. Dip the tiles with terracotta slip into white slip, immersing the face of the tile and the still-embedded leaf. Dip the tiles with leaves impressed into the raw clay into terracotta slip. Set aside to dry back to leather-hard. Smooth the surfaces with the edge of a steel palette.

With the point of a potter's needle, carefully lift the stem of each leaf and gently ease it away from the tile to reveal the contrasting color underneath and a perfect skeletal leaf. Clean up any detail, where the slip might have seeped behind the leaf, with a craft knife. True up the edges with a surform, then sponge smooth. Allow to fully dry and then bisque fire to 2050°F (1120°C).

When cold, remove the tiles from the kiln and ensure that the surfaces are completely dust free. Dip the white tiles with terracotta leaves into the transparent glaze and the terracotta tiles with the white leaves into the amber glaze.

Allow the glazes to dry, then carefully clean off any excess glaze from the backs with a damp sponge. Fire to 1940-1980°F (1060-1080°C).

nefertem frieze

I used three different colors on this sgraffito panel and found it very satisfying to watch the panel come to life as if by magic. Scraping away to reveal the colors below becomes compulsive – you are always at a stage where you cannot wait to move on to the next tile! This panel design is based on the Egyptian lotus – a flower associated with Nefertem, the god of creativity. Don't feel obliged to directly copy this design, which was the result of a morning's research at the British Museum and an afternoon in my local library. With a little research you're sure to come up with a stunning alternative.

skills required
- ❑ rolling out, page 12
- ❑ cutting out, page 14
- ❑ decorating slip, page 20
- ❑ drying out, page 15
- ❑ bisque firing, page 24
- ❑ mixing and applying glaze, page 22
- ❑ bisque and glaze firing, page 24

equipment:
rolling pin, rolling guides, calico cloth, batts,
pencil or ballpoint pen, tracing paper,
steel ruler, pair of compasses,
4 in (100 mm) tile cutter or template,
craft knife, potter's needle,
small-bladed screwdriver, metal kidney,
small fan brush, small paintbrush,
paint tray, surform, bowl, water, sponge

clay and glaze:
to make about 16 tiles, each 4 in (100 mm)
square, you will need 20 lb (10 kg) white
earthenware clay, 1 pt (500 ml) white decorating slip,
1 pt (500 ml) terracotta decorating slip, 2 lb (1 kg) lead-
free earthenware transparent glaze, 1 fl oz (25 ml)
quantities of ready-mixed underglaze in lavender, dark
green, light green and yellow

PREPARATION Draw out the main features, then lay out a
full-size grid on tracing paper and trace the chosen motifs
into the relevant positions. At this stage consider the

number of colors and their separation. If you want to use
bands of color you will have to plan which color is to be laid
on first.

Prepare, roll and cut out 16 tiles (from these you will
have your complete panel). Transfer the design from your
tracing on to the tiles and leave to dry to soft leather.

Cut six tiles in half using a ruler and craft knife to make
the border tiles and cut one tile into quarters to make the
corners. Be as accurate in your cutting and measuring as

This richly colored piece would look equally good mounted as an interior wall panel or inset into a worktop.

possible. Leave all the tiles to dry to leather-hard. When leather-hard, dip all the tiles into the terracotta slip and leave once more to return to the leather-hard state.

Give the border and corner tiles a secondary dip in the white slip. Place them carefully on a batt and leave once more to return to leather-hard.

CENTRAL DESIGN Starting with the nine terracotta tiles, take a ballpoint pen and draw a wavy border, removing the terracotta to reveal the white underneath. The dry slip will just fall off as the pen passes over it. (If you don't achieve a clean line let the tiles dry a little more.)

Next, use a pair of compasses with the pencil lead removed and work on the three roundels at the center of each of the top tiles to make a clean circle. Draw the petal forms inside the circles then, with a screwdriver blade, remove the area between the petals.

Move down the panel and work on the lotus flowers with a ballpoint to gradually reveal their forms. Define the petals and the finer detailing around the bases with a potter's needle. Remove all the terracotta on the secondary petals by using a metal kidney or screwdriver. They will be colored in later.

BORDER DESIGN Now work on the border and corner tiles. As before, define the wavy border, taking care that it matches up with border on the tiles either side. Take care only to remove the white slip. (If you press too hard you will also remove the terracotta slip beneath the white.) Load a fan brush with lavender underglaze and cover

the borders up to the wavy line to change the color of the border easily. Touch in with a fine paintbrush and leave to dry.

Starting with the corners, use a compass and screwdriver to remove the lavender from the edges and petals of the roundels, defining all detailing with the potter's needle. Now carefully scrape away the white as shown on page 43.

The scarabs and palm leaves are next. Lay the tiles together and, with a ballpoint pen, define the outlines of the scarab wings, making sure that they match up. Move on to the scarabs' bodies. Define the heads by removing the areas of lavender and detail the eyes with a ball-point. Outline the stripes of the bodies in terracotta and alternate them by scraping the lavender away.

Heavily define the outline shapes of the palms to reveal the terracotta and, with a finer line, draw the veins. Use a metal kidney to scrape away the lavender from the stalks and alternate the veins on either side with white and lavender – it is not necessary for each leaf to be identical.

ASSEMBLY Assemble the panel and carefully color the petals and stalks of the lotus flowers with yellow, greens and lavender. Touch up any mistakes with the relevant color and define any missed bits. Brush off any scraps of waste and leave to become bone dry. Bisque fire to 1830°F (1000°C).

Remove from the kiln and brush off any dust. Dip in the transparent glaze, wipe the backs and fire to 1940-1980°F (1060-1080°C).

market garden

These stylized fruit and vegetable tiles will create a bright, crisp feel for your kitchen splashback or work surface. For design ideas look at contemporary items in your local kitchen equipment store. Once you have decided on the motifs to use you will need to draw their outlines on to thin card and cut a template for each motif. Each motif template will have to be scaled to sit neatly within the square. So a strawberry will need to be larger than life-size but a watermelon will, of course, have to be considerably smaller!

skills required
❑ rolling out, page 12
❑ cutting out, page 14
❑ drying out, page 15
❑ underglaze, page 20
❑ mixing and applying glaze, page 22
❑ bisque firing, page 24
❑ glaze firing, page 24

you will need:
rolling pin, guides, calico, batts,
4 in (100 mm) tile cutter or template,
paintbrushes, stiff toothbrush, card templates,
pencil or ballpoint pen, craft knife, potter's needle,
surform, bowl, water, sponge, paint tray

clay and glaze:
to make about 40 tiles you will need 40 lb (20 kg) white
earthenware clay, 2½ fl oz (60 ml) quantities of ready-
mixed underglaze in dark green, light green, bright
yellow, orange, red, white and maroon, 10 fl oz
(250 ml) wax-resist emulsion, 4 lb (2 kg) lead-free
transparent glaze

PREPARATION Before starting, you need to work out
how many triangular tiles to make to fill in the
spaces at the top, bottom and sides. Remember to
allow for a grout line between each tile. Prepare and
cut your tiles and leave to dry to leather-hard. True up
with a surform, paying attention to the 45 degree
angles. Clean up with a damp sponge.

You needn't limit yourself to the three motifs shown – try your hand at a whole range of fruit and veg – celery, onions, watermelon slices and tomatoes all work equally well.

DECORATION Decorate each tile with a different fruit or vegetable. Below is an eggplant decoration, for example. Draw this simple shape on some card and cut out to provide yourself with a template. Lay a tile diagonally in front of you, place your template in the center and lightly draw around it. Color the body of the eggplant with maroon underglaze. Use long strokes from top to bottom following the curve of the vegetable. Apply a slightly thicker coat on one side and highlight the center with a little white. With a ballpoint pen, incise a curved line down the side to accentuate the shape. Color the stalk with dark green and leave to dry. Incise the outline of the stalk and body of the eggplant. Next paint over the motif and the white outline with wax resist (see page 48 for details). Leave to dry. Don't forget to rinse out your brush before the wax dries!

Coat the background with pale green underglaze. (It doesn't matter if you go over the motif as the wax resist acts as a mask.) With a fine brush, lay intermittent strokes of dark green diagonally across the tile. Take the potter's needle and in the same direction incise fine lines across the tile to remove areas of dark and light green. Leave to dry completely. Move on to the next tile.

Using the same method, decorate the other fruit with appropriate colors.

BORDER AND PLAIN TILES While the motifs are drying out, work on the borders of the plain square and triangular tiles. Load a small flat-edged or shader brush with dark green underglaze and paint a band of color all the way around. Allow it to dry. With a potter's needle, crosshatch into the green to reveal white lines. Blow away any waste and leave to dry out.

Bisque fire to 1830°F (1000°C). Remove from the kiln and with a toothbrush remove any loose bits of clay or color. Dip the tiles into transparent glaze, wipe the backs and allow to dry. Glaze fire to 1940-1980°F (1060-1080°C).

Stamping, sponging and wax resist are all paint-effect techniques. They are relatively quick and easy to do, so are an excellent way to cover a large area of tiling effectively.

Stamping involves pressing into soft or leather-hard clay to alter the surface texture. You can use items such as printers' letters, or wooden stamps (see Tribute to Delft, page 50) – these can be found in craft markets – wooden beading, the edges of coins or almost any other object. By rolling and pressing flat objects such as leaves, lace and netting, you can create interesting patterns and textures. To take full advantage of this technique you should use a colored transparent glaze that will pool into the impressions, enhance the detailing and give variations in color intensity to your tiles.

Sponging is another paint-effect technique that works well on tiles – all you need is a sponge and some colorful glaze.

Wax-resist emulsion is used as a mask and is sold in tubs ready to use. Whatever areas are covered with the wax-resist will not take the color painted on top. It allows you to decorate overlaying colors to give crisp outlines on contrasting backgrounds. It can also be used on the edges of tiles to ensure there is no overrun of glaze – which can make laying and grouting the finished tiles a frustrating business. Apply wax-resist with an old paintbrush and clean your brush afterwards with very hot water and detergent.

golden panel

For these tiles I have used an embossed wallpaper border with a repeat pattern. You can either adapt the design to fit the tile or make the tile to suit the design. You can also take details of the pattern to decorate individual tiles. By judicious use of the detail, you break up the expanse of field tiles without over-decorating them.

skills required
- ❑ rolling out, page 12
- ❑ cutting out, page 14
- ❑ drying out, page 15
- ❑ mixing and applying glaze, page 22
- ❑ bisque firing, page 24
- ❑ glaze firing, page 24

equipment:
rolling pin, rolling guides, calico, batts,
4 in (100 mm) square tile cutter or template,
4 x $7\frac{3}{4}$ in (100 x 197 mm) template,
3 ft (1 m) embossed wallpaper border (hardware stores give free samples), craft knife or potter's knife, potter's needle, surform, scissors, paint tray and roller, bowl, water, sponge

clay:
To make 10 tiles 4 x $7\frac{3}{4}$ in (100 x 197 mm) and 20 tiles 4 in (100 mm) square you will need 40lb (20 kg) white earthenware clay

to make the glazes:
2 fl oz (60 ml) dark green, ready-mixed underglaze
1 oz (25 g) of rutile or dark yellow powder underglaze mixed with 1 pt (500 ml) water
4 lb (2 kg) mid-temperature, transparent, lead-free glaze

Measure and cut your wallpaper to fit the 4 x 7¾ in (100 x 197 mm) tiles and cut a section to fit on the square tiles. Prepare, roll out and cut all your tiles, leave to dry leather-hard and then true and clean up. Lay out as many tiles as will fit on your work surface, with the 4 x 7¾ in (100 x 197 mm) tiles along the top.

Pour the mixed rutile or underglaze into the paint tray and mix. (You will have to stir it every 5–10 minutes as the rutile tends to settle on the bottom.) Dip the roller into the pigment and roll it on to all the tiles. Don't worry if it looks patchy – the idea is to create a variation in the color.

Dilute, if necessary, the dark green underglaze to the consistency of single cream and pour into the paint tray. Take a 4 x 7¾ in (100 x 197 mm) tile and the piece of wallpaper cut to size. Lay the wallpaper on to newspaper with the embossed face uppermost. Dip the roller into the underglaze and gently roll it on to the raised surface of the wallpaper, ensuring that all the detail is covered. Carefully position the paper square to the edge of the tile and gently,

but firmly, apply even pressure with the palm of your hand to transfer the color. Peel away the paper to reveal the pattern on the tile, as shown. Repeat for all the border tiles.

Work out how many square tiles you want to decorate. (One in six is quite effective.) Using the same method as described above, decorate these tiles by placing the motif in the center. Allow all the tiles to dry out. Bisque fire to 1830°F (1000°C).

Remove the tiles from the kiln and brush off any dust. Dip the tiles in transparent glaze, allow to dry and wipe the backs clean. Glaze fire to 1940–1980°F (1060-1080°C).

Using a paint tray and a 4 in (100 mm) decorator's roller, I rolled the yellow underglaze straight on to the tiles – as if painting a color wash on to a wall, then I rolled the underglaze directly on to the wallpaper and printed it on to the tiles.

The possibilities for animal designs are limited only by your ability to obtain a variety of animal stamps.

tribute to delft

These animal motifs are based on traditional Delft tiles. Using wooden printing blocks with color is an easy and effective way to create painted animals without having to draw. The plastic cap of a felt pen served as a stamp for the floral connecting motif in the corner of each tile. The small corner design will pull the tile panel together. To create a border, I sprigged on a small moulding by building up multiple extrusions from a clay gun.

skills required
- ❏ rolling out, page 12
- ❏ cutting out, page 14
- ❏ drying out, page 15
- ❏ plaster casting and making sprigs, page 17
- ❏ using a clay gun, page 19
- ❏ mixing and applying glaze, page 22
- ❏ bisque and glaze firing, page 24

equipment:
rolling pin, guides, calico, batts, clay gun, toothbrush,
4 in (100 mm) square tile cutter or template,
craft knife or potter's knife, potter's needle, fine paintbrush,
animal wooden stamps, small stamp for the corner patterns,
bowl, water, sponge, surform

clay:
To make 10 border tiles and 20 decorated tiles you will
    need 30 lb (15 kg) white earthenware clay

to make the glazes:
2 fl oz (60 ml) medium blue ready-mixed underglaze
4 lb (2 kg) transparent medium-temperature lead-free glaze

Prepare, roll out and cut your tiles. Leave the 20 that will be stamped to dry to soft leather and allow the border tiles to become leather-hard.

ANIMALS Paint the wooden animal stamp with underglaze, as shown. Press the block into the center of the tile to transfer the color and the imprint of the animal. Place the tile under polythene and decorate a further nine tiles with, for example, rabbits and the remaining 10 with, say, birds.

BORDER With a half-round die fitted to the clay gun, extrude lengths of beading. Place the beading on one of the border tiles and cut to size. Set aside the beading. Score and dampen the surface of the tile, press the beading in place and wipe away any excess. Decorate all the border tiles in this manner.

CORNER MOTIFS Lay out all the tiles with the border tiles at the top. Dip the small stamp into the underglaze and press into the corners of all the tiles. Using the edge of a wire modelling tool dipped in underglaze, make a diagonal line into the corner of the tile to create a cross pattern that will link the tiles together.

Allow to become leather-hard again, true with a surform and carefully sponge the edges clean. Leave the tiles to dry out fully. Bisque fire to 1830°F (1000°C). Remove from the kiln and brush off any dust, dip in the transparent glaze, allow to dry and wipe the edges and backs clean. Glaze fire to 1940–1980°F (1060–1080°C).

daisy chain

Here, a simple daisy motif is used to striking effect in the center of each tile – with a leaf set inside a corner triangle to unite each tile. The border features larger leaves with daisies set in the smaller corner tiles. The underglazes have been watered down and used like watercolor paint, with wax-resist emulsion to keep a white ground as well as acting as a mask. Always allow the wax to dry before applying color and regularly rinse your brush as you work, to avoid a build-up of wax which will start to solidify.

skills required
❑ rolling out, page 12
❑ cutting out, page 14
❑ drying out, page 15
❑ underglaze, page 20
❑ mixing and applying glaze, page 22
❑ bisque firing, page 24
❑ glaze firing, page 24

equipment:
rolling pin, guides, calico, ballpoint pen,
4 in (100 mm) square tile cutter or template,
cardboard templates based on photograph opposite of
5-petal daisy 2 in (50 mm) wide and square $2\frac{3}{4}$ in (70 mm),
fine paintbrush, old fine paintbrush (for the wax resist),
paint tray, craft knife or potter's knife, potter's needle,
steel ruler, bowl, water, sponge, coarse toothbrush

clay:
To make 34 tiles 4 in (100 mm) square, 10 tiles 2 x 4 in
(50 x 100 mm) and 4 tiles 2 in (50 mm) square you will
need 30 lb (15 kg) white earthenware clay.

to make the glazes:
2 fl oz (60 ml) quantities each of underglaze in lilac, dark
green, bright yellow, turquoise and dark blue, 1 pt (500
ml) wax-resist emulsion, 4 lb (2 kg) mid-temperature
transparent lead-free glaze

DESIGN Prepare, roll out and cut all your tiles and leave to dry to leather-hard. Apply a thin band of wax resist all the way around the outer edge of the tiles and leave the wax to dry. Working on the 4 in (100 mm) square tiles first, position the $2\frac{3}{4}$ in (70 mm) card template diagonally in the center to form a diamond and paint around it with the wax. Place the daisy silhouette in the center of the diamond and wax around the outline. Remove the template, carefully define each petal and paint a small circle in the center with the wax resist. Rinse your brush.

Color the center of the daisy with the lilac underglaze, allow it to dry and cover with wax. Wash the daisy petals with yellow underglaze and cover with wax. Color the diamonds behind the daisies with turquoise underglaze.

In the corner triangles, paint the outline of a leaf with the wax, color the centers with dark green and with the ball-point pen, incise a small vein along its length. Cover the leaf with wax. Apply dark blue behind the green leaves. The tiles are now ready to dry out fully.

Decorate the small corner squares with a yellow daisy and a turquoise background in the same way. On the border tiles paint two leaf shapes with the wax resist, color with the dark green and coat with wax. Finally, put a wash of dark blue behind the leaves to match the square tiles.

FIRING All the tiles are now ready to dry out. Bisque fire to 1830°F (1000°C). Remove from the kiln and – with a toothbrush – remove any residue of wax and underglaze. Dip the tiles into the transparent glaze and leave to dry, then wipe the sides and backs. Glaze fire to 1940–1980°F (1060–1080°C).

Simple forms, such as this daisy and leaf motif, are both colorful and pleasing. Many other similar forms would lend themselves to this wax-resist technique – how about moons and stars or hearts and arrows?

A sponge effect is the perfect technique to emphasise the delicate texture of a butterfly's wing.

butterfly tiles

These plain white tiles are decorated using a hand-cut sponge dipped into blue glaze which is then printed on to a tile that has been coated in a white glaze. I have chosen a butterfly motif, but you could, of course, design and cut your own motif or buy one ready-made from a decorating shop.

skills required
- ❏ rolling out, page 12
- ❏ cutting out, page 14
- ❏ drying out, page 15
- ❏ mixing and applying glaze, page 22
- ❏ bisque and glaze firing, page 24

equipment:
rolling pin, guides, calico, batts,
4 in (100 mm) square tile cutter or template,
scissors, craft knife, potter's needle, permanent marker,
surform, cellulose sponge about 3¼ x 2½ in (8 x 6.5 cm),
paint tray, shader paintbrush (size 6), fine paintbrush (size 8),
bowl, water, sponge

clay and glaze:
to make 40 bisque tiles 4 in (100 mm) square you will need (40 lb) 20 kg white earthenware clay and (4 lb) 2 kg shiny white earthenware glaze

to make the glazes:
2 fl oz (60 ml) opaque yellow brush-on glaze
2 fl oz (60 ml) quantities transparent brush-on glaze in dark blue and dark green

DESIGN Prepare, roll and cut out all your tiles and leave to dry till leather-hard. Clean and true with a surform; leave to dry. Bisque fire to 1830°F (1000°C).

Draw the outline of a butterfly on to a sponge. Cut away the background with a craft knife or scissors, leaving the butterfly to stand proud.

GLAZING & FIRING Ensure that your tiles are free from dust and dip them into the white glaze. Leave to dry. Pour the glaze back into its container and cover. (It is very frustrating to find a speck of color on a pure white, fired tile.)

Clean out the paint tray, pour in half of the dark blue glaze and dilute with a little water. Take the cut sponge and dip it into the glaze, position it in the center of the tile and press lightly. If you press too hard the glaze will run, resulting in a blurred image.

Decorate half your tiles with a butterfly motif. Scratch away a circle of blue to form the eyes on the wings. Load a small brush with yellow and blob into the recess.

Using the shader brush and the dark blue glaze, paint a band of glaze around the edge of each tile. Clean the brush and paint a stripe of dark green in between the butterfly's wings to represent its body. With a loaded brush, blob the dark green on top of the blue band at the corners. Add three more blobs, equally spaced along each edge. Wipe the backs of the tiles with a damp sponge. Glaze fire to 1940–1980°F (1060–1080°C).

ONGLAZE & LUSTER

this section deals with what is usually the final stage in commercial tile making before the tiles are graded and packed. Onglaze and luster are both quick and simple methods – in most cases – of adding color to a plain background. This chapter also reveals an amazing discovery I made while in my studio working on a totally different project – not ceramics at all. Enough of that for now, except to say that in the Gilded Quarry Tile project (see page 59), all will be revealed!

Onglaze is available as a water-based or oil-based product. Obviously you should not mix the two types. It is a slightly viscous painting medium, easy to control with a reasonable range of colors and comes in powder form or small ready-mixed pots. Most of the French porcelain from Limoges is painted in this fashion.

Luster is a gold, platinum or any other metallic or iridescent finish. Again, these can be bought in different media and are applied by brush.

There are a number of new products available that have considerably reduced the cost of adding 'gold' to your work. Some of these are water-based and therefore similar to acrylic paints. They tend to give a matt surface which is I think, in many cases, more attractive than a traditional bright and shiny gold.

rococo relief

For this relief, I have chosen an ornate sprig taken from an elaborate escutcheon plate that lends itself well to this rather ornate gilding. You could use this project to practise applying luster to bought-in tiles. However, if you do, consider carefully the color of the tiles you buy and the type of luster you intend to apply. It is all too easy when using luster, to 'over-gild the lily' and end up with a vulgar travesty. Beware of using glazes with a high copper content as the base for your work. Luster has a tendency to blacken in conjunction with copper glazes and can also cause bright gold to turn brown.

skills required
- ❏ rolling out, page 12
- ❏ cutting out, page 14
- ❏ drying out, page 15
- ❏ plaster casting and making sprigs, page 17
- ❏ mixing and applying glaze, page 22
- ❏ bisque and glaze firing, page 24

equipment:
rococo ornament to cast, rolling pin, guides, calico, batts, 4 in (100 mm) tile cutter or template, craft knife, potter's needle, bowl, water, sponge, rubber gloves, plaster, surform, fine paintbrush, plastic scraper or old credit card

clay:
to make 10 ornate tiles and 30 field tiles you will need
30 lb (15 kg) white earthenware clay

to make the dark blue glaze for the ornate tiles:
13 oz (375 g) high-alkaline frit (see glossary, page 77)
3 oz (75 g) china clay
2 oz (50 g) flint
$\frac{1}{4}$ oz (5 g) cobalt carbonate
$\frac{1}{4}$ oz (5 g) copper carbonate
1 pt (500 ml) of water

I recommend bright gold for this application. It is expensive but you do not need very much to make a substantial impact.

to make the dark green glaze for the field tiles:

1 lb 10 oz (750 g) high-alkaline frit

6 oz (150 g) china clay

4 oz (100 g) flint

$\frac{3}{4}$ oz (20 g) copper carbonate

$\frac{1}{4}$ oz (5 g) cobalt carbonate

2 pt (1 liter) of water

Weigh out the above ingredients, mix with the water and sieve through an 80-mesh sieve.

for painting details on to the glazes:

$\frac{1}{4}$ oz (5 g) bright gold luster

2 fl oz (50 ml) luster thinners

Prepare and cut your tiles and leave to dry leather-hard. Make and apply the sprigs on to 10 of the tiles. True all of the tiles and sponge them clean. Leave to dry slowly and bisque fire to 1830°F (1000°C).

Remove the tiles from the kiln and brush away any dust. Dip the field tiles into the green glaze and the ornate tiles into the blue glaze. Leave to dry and wipe the backs clean. Glaze fire to 1940°F (1060°C).

Remove the tiles from the kiln. Do not handle the faces of the tiles with your fingers as body oils will prevent the luster adhering to the glaze. If you are concerned, wipe the faces of the ornate tiles over with some white spirit on a soft cloth. Allow the spirit to evaporate before proceeding.

Using a fine brush, apply the luster with even strokes, picking out some of the detailing as shown. If the luster is too thick and does not flow well add some thinners. (Don't add too much, as the luster will not fire to bright gold if it is too thin.)

Leave to dry and wash your brush thoroughly in the thinners. Re-fire as for a glaze firing, but only to 1400°F (760°C). Remember to ventilate your studio well.

gilded quarry tiles

This project is where I reveal my exciting discovery – these hard-wearing floor tiles require no glazing! Instead they are protected by two-part epoxy resin – a common glue – which is now so advanced that it can emulate the properties of glaze without the need for a glaze firing. I have not tested this material in extreme conditions or over an extended period of time, but for domestic purposes it seems admirable. Before using such resin, please read the manufacturer's specification sheet as the chemical changes that take place can be affected by factors such as ambient temperature. If there is a down side to this product, it is that in direct sunlight it yellows. However, if necessary, you can apply a UV protection product after the sealer has fully cured.

materials and equipment:
hard pencil, steel ruler, pair of compasses,
coin or disc $\frac{3}{4}$ in (20 mm) diameter,
shader brushes (sizes 6, 10 and 12),
fine paintbrushes (sizes 6 and 8),
bowl, water, 12 in (300 mm) square quarry tiles,
2 fine permanent gold pens,
metallic craft acrylic paints:
    2 fl oz (59 ml) Royal Ruby (x 2),
    2 fl oz (59 ml) quantities of Venetian Gold
      and Glorious Gold
tube of gold glass contour paste

to apply the sealer:
two-part epoxy resin – system 320 or equivalent
    (2 fl oz/7 ml per tile)
cheap or old $\frac{1}{2}$ in (12 mm) decorator's brush
rubber gloves
small plastic pot
wooden spatula
2 small measuring syringes

DESIGN With a sharp pencil and steel ruler divide each tile into four sections. Using the gold pen and ruler, draw a border 1 in (25 mm) in from the edge on all four sides to form four corner squares. From the middle of each edge, draw a line 1½ in (40 mm) long into the center of the tile and color with the gold pen. Connect the lines together to form a diamond in the center.

In each of the corners, draw around a $\frac{3}{4}$ in (20 mm) coin or disc with the gold pen. Inside the border draw four more circles equally spaced on each side of the tile. Draw a $\frac{1}{8}$ in (2 mm) disc in the center of each circle. In the center of the tile draw a circle 2 in (50 mm) in diameter and divide it into four. Outline the circle and dividing lines with a gold pen. Draw a quatrefoil 1 in (25 mm) across in the center of the circle. Use glass paste to give a raised line to outline the quatrefoil and leave it to dry. Again, use glass paste to draw four scrolls in each of the quarters running parallel with the gold line of the diamond and leave to dry.

COLOR Use a large shader brush and the Royal Ruby color to paint the large triangle of each corner section of the tile.

Paint up to the gold line. Use a small brush and Royal Ruby to color the background behind the circles in the corner squares of the border. Use Glorious Gold to color the background of the border behind the circles and the quatrefoil in the center. Use Venetian Gold to color in the background of the center circle behind the scrolls. When dry, the tile is now ready to be sealed.

A very simple, yet stunning, geometric pattern is given an instant glaze with two-part epoxy resin.

Here, the design of the tile is shown complete for your reference.

SEALANT Wearing rubber gloves, take the two-part epoxy resin sealer and use the syringes that are supplied to measure out accurately 2 fl oz (7 ml) per tile. The mix ratio may differ from one manufacturer to another. It is essential that the manufacturer's instructions are followed exactly, otherwise you may find that the resin does not react properly and it will not provide the protection it should.

When thoroughly mixed, pour a small amount of resin on to each tile, spread out with a spatula and finally touch in with an old brush. Work quickly, as the setting time is about 25 minutes per mix. When finished you will have to dispose of the brush.

house number plaque

One of the simplest aspects of ceramics is the use of onglaze, or enamelware as it is sometimes known. If you can draw or paint a simple design on paper, it is easy enough to transfer your design on to a ceramic tile or, for that matter, anything else that has a pre-glazed background. Most of the decorated ceramic ware on the mass market is produced using this technique. The design here is based on a dress fabric pattern with the numbers taken from a standard 'alphabet' and then blown up to size.

skills required
❑ low-temperature glaze firing,
   page 24

materials and equipment:
pencil, tracing paper,
masking tape, tile cutter,
fine paintbrushes, bowl, water,
kitchen paper, 3 white 6 in
(150 mm) square tiles

to make the glaze:
water-based onglaze in black, red
   and yellow

PREPARATION Work out the size of your plaque and cut the tiles to size. If using more than two tiles (ie, you have three or more figures which make up your house number), cut both edges of the center tile(s). Ensure that all the tiles are free from grease and dust before you begin.

NUMBERS Trace your numerals and go over the outline on the reverse side of the tracing paper with a pencil. Position each numeral individually on to each tile with a piece of masking tape.

An adaptable design, you can use one, two, three or more tiles to make your own house number.

Carefully outline the numeral with the pencil to transfer the design on to the tile.

Outline the number with the black onglaze using a well-loaded brush. Fill in with black, using even strokes to obtain a flat color. Leave to dry and repeat on the next, and any subsequent tiles. Clean the brushes thoroughly and dry with kitchen paper.

FLOWERS When the black onglaze is completely dry, reposition the tiles together and mark out the flower design using the same method as above (although it is quite easy to reproduce this type of design freehand).

Color in the yellow petals first, using two brushstrokes side by side. Allow the yellow to dry before proceeding with the next color. Use a loaded brush to dot the red onglaze in the center of each flower. Once again allow to dry completely.

With a very fine paintbrush outline the petals in black using quick light strokes, then leave to dry. Touch up any patchy or irregular lines with the appropriate color and clean up any mistakes or smudges with a piece of kitchen paper.

FIRING Fire in the same way as a glaze firing, but only to 1700°F (800°C).

Gold luster adds an exotic sparkle to the central motif, being based on Indian fretwork.
These tiles could well form the basis for a room decorated in an ethnic, Eastern style.

sari sari

These tiles have a repeat floral pattern that seemed to lend itself to a stencilled design. Half- and quarter-motifs are used on the edges and corners to complete the pattern when all the tiles are joined together. Either make your own white tiles or buy ready-made ones and decorate them. If you do buy the tiles, look for ones that have a handmade appearance, such as those made in Portugal, Spain or Italy. Fix on any tiled surface or just loose-lay as a scatter decoration. These tiles can even be sited in a shower.

equipment:
pencil, paper, stencil card, small stencil brush, craft knife, masking tape, fine paintbrush

clay and glaze:
to make and glaze 30 tiles you will need 20 lb (10 kg) white earthenware clay, 3 lb (1.5 kg) shiny white earthenware glaze

to decorate the tiles:
$\frac{1}{2}$ fl oz (10 ml) red ready-mixed onglaze
$\frac{1}{8}$ oz (5 g) bright gold luster
2 fl oz (50 ml) luster thinners

BASIC TILES Prepare and cut 30 tiles, then leave to dry to leather-hard. True all the tiles and sponge clean. Leave to dry slowly and bisque fire to 1830°F (1000°C). Remove from the kiln and brush away any dust. Dip all of the tiles into the white glaze. Leave to dry and wipe the backs clean. Glaze fire to 1940°F (1060°C). Remove the tiles from the kiln, taking care not to handle the fronts.

DESIGN Draw your design on to paper, cut a square piece of stencil paper the same size as your tile and transfer your design on to it. Cut out the areas to be colored with a very sharp craft knife or scalpel to obtain a clean edge.

Lay the stencil squarely on to the tile and secure with small pieces of masking tape. Dip a stencil brush into the red onglaze, press the stencil down with your left hand to prevent the color getting behind the stencil and dab into the cut-out design. Start at the top and work clockwise to prevent smudging the onglaze with your hand. Carefully

remove the stencil from the tile. Wipe off any smears with a piece of damp kitchen paper.

When all the red has been applied and the tiles are dry, you can paint the bright gold luster on to them. Load the fine brush with the luster and carefully outline the central motif. Clean your brush with the thinners.

Once all the tiles are finished, place them in the kiln and fire to 1400°F (760°C).

a n ancient method of introducing a distinguishing feature to a tiled installation is by using a repeat geometric pattern. Sometimes these patterns are of a quite dazzling complexity. One of the more famous examples of geometric patterning is the Moorish tiling installed in Spain in the 15th century. These patterns are called 'Mudejar' after the craftsmen or 'mudejares' who designed and installed them. Their method was interesting because they made large slabs of glazed clay and then cut them into shapes after firing, to ensure a greater accuracy and better fit.

In Morocco there has recently been a huge resurgence of this – what had become a dying – skill. King Hussan instigated a training programme in the early 1960s and now Morocco leads the Islamic world in producing vast wall installations of stunning intricacy.

Another method of introducing variety is the use of tacos – small square tiles of a size divisible from the larger field tiles. They are used in a design that shifts the pattern to one side. They are also known as insets or inserts.

modern medieval

The design of these shaped tiles was inspired by 19th-century copies of medieval floor tiles laid as a mosaic pattern in the Chappelle de St. Cucuphas in Saint-Denis in Paris. The color scheme is taken from the lush mosaic panels of the Palace of the Alhambra in Granada in southern Spain. I've used a pastry cutter to create the quatrefoil.

skills required
❑ rolling out, page 12
❑ cutting out, page 14
❑ drying out, page 15
❑ mixing and applying glaze, page 22
❑ bisque firing, page 24
❑ glaze firing, page 24

equipment:
rolling pin, guides, calico, batts,
2¾ in (70 mm) pastry cutter,
4 in (100 mm) square tile cutter or template,
steel square, craft knife, potter's needle,
bowl, water, sponge,
small mop or fan brush,

clay:
To make 60 tiles you will need 40 lb (20 kg) white earthenware clay

to make the glazes:
4 fl oz (100 ml) opaque bright yellow brush-on earthenware glaze

2 fl oz (60 ml) quantities of opaque brush-on earthenware glaze in medium blue and purple

2 fl oz (60 ml) transparent turquoise brush-on earthenware glaze

CUTTING THE PATTERN Prepare and cut your 4 in (100 mm) tiles and leave until soft leather-hard. Lay the tiles out together and remove the centers with a pastry

This interlocking pattern of bright hues would look vibrant in a modern setting where geometric shapes and primary colors predominate.

cutter to form the quatrefoils. Carefully lay them in the order you have cut them on a separate board. Leave both parts of the tiles to dry to leather-hard, clean up any blurred edges from the quatrefoils with a sharp craft knife, round off the edges and clean the faces of all the tiles with a damp sponge.

Re-assemble both parts of the tiles, working in batches of 10. Lay a steel square on top of the tiles and mark the center of the quatrefoils horizontally on the outside piece of the tile. Rotate square and mark the vertical line. Remove the quatrefoil and, holding the square firmly in place, cut down the center of the tiles from top to bottom. Lay the square horizontally across the tiles and cut into quarters. Using a knife, surform and damp sponge clean up the edges. Re-assemble the tiles with the quatrefoils in the center and leave to dry.

GLAZING AND FIRING Pack the tiles on to the kiln shelves, assembled to keep all the pieces together. This helps to ensure a good fit later on. Bisque fire to 1830°F (1000°C).

Remove from the kiln and brush off any dust. Apply the glazes one color at a time, starting with yellow. Load a fan brush and — with even strokes — brush the glaze on to 30 quatrefoils and 20 sets of quarter tiles. Clean the brush and apply turquoise to the remaining 30 quatrefoils. Brush mid-blue on to 20 sets of quarter tiles and purple on to the remaining 20 sets of quarter tiles. Clean up the edges and backs with a damp sponge. Pack on to the kiln shelves, keeping the quarter tiles in their sets, but ensure that the tiles are not touching. Glaze fire to 1920–1940°F (1050–1060°C). Allow the kiln to cool, then unpack the tiles. Assemble them prior to fixing in position.

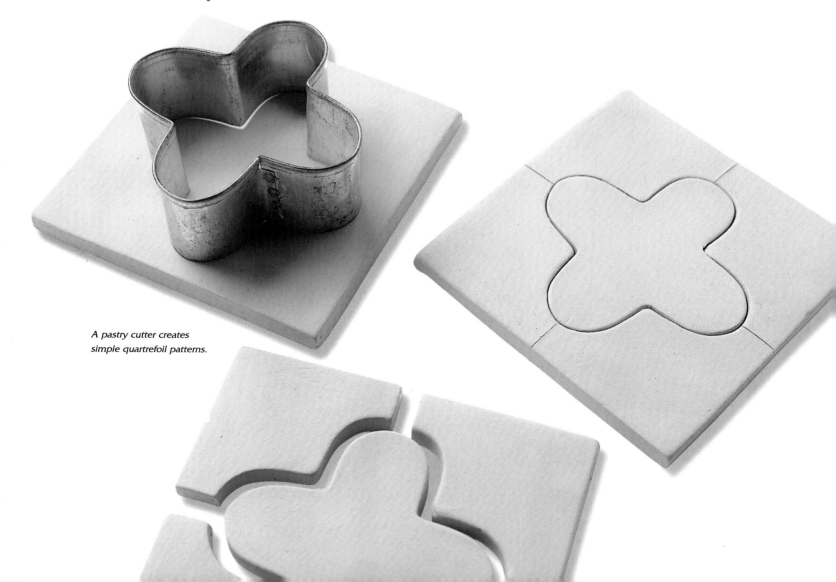

A pastry cutter creates simple quartrefoil patterns.

star panel

In this panel, tacos are used to create an attractive, inlaid star pattern. Inlay work is the technique of removing a swath of clay from a basic shape and then filling the incision with a similar clay of a contrasting color. It is important that the two clays are of the same type and that the depth of the incision is kept to a minimum. This will reduce the problems of two differing clays shrinking at variable rates. The key to successful inlay work is in letting your tiles dry out slowly. Be patient!

skills required
- ❏ wedging, page 12
- ❏ rolling out, page 12
- ❏ cutting out, page 14
- ❏ drying out, page 15
- ❏ mixing and applying glaze, page 22
- ❏ bisque and glaze firing, page 24

equipment:
batts, cardboard templates of star 1 in (30 mm) wide,
rectangle 4 x 8 in (100 x 200 mm), square 2 in (50 mm),
calico, rolling pin, guides, strong plastic bag, paint tray,
craft knife or potter's knife, potter's needle,
bowl, water, sponge, steel palette, wire modelling tool

clay and stain:
To make about 15 black tiles with white inlay and 15 white with
black inlay 2 in (50 mm) square inset tiles you will need
2 lb (1 kg) dry white earthenware clay, 4 oz (100 g) black body stain.
To make thirty 4 x 8 in (100 x 200 mm) tiles you will need 50 lb (25 kg)
white earthenware clay

glaze:
For thirty 4 x 8 in (100 x 200 mm) square tiles you will need
4 lb (2 kg) matt cream earthenware glaze

TILES Prepare and roll out the white earthenware. Use the rectangular template to cut out 40 tiles. Use the square template to cut out the white insets and wrap them well in polythene to be inlaid with black later. Dry out the rest of the tiles to leather-hard, true with the surform and sponge clean. Leave to dry out and bisque fire to 1830°F (1000°C).

BLACK CLAY Weigh out the dry clay and black body stain, place it in a plastic bag and secure (to avoid making too much dust). Gently crush it with a rolling pin to break the

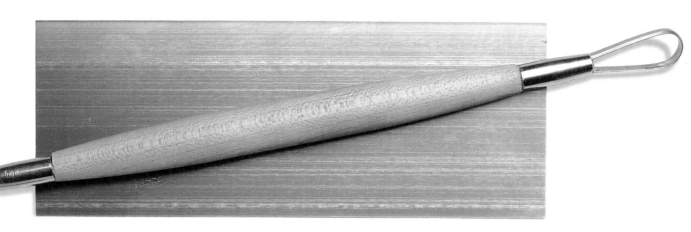

A steel palette and a wire modeller: remove and smooth with these two tools.

clay into small pieces and shake the bag to mix the clay and pigment together. Carefully pour into a bowl, avoiding making dust. Cover the mixture with water and leave to stand for at least six hours so that the clay can completely break down.

Once dissolved, let your mix dry out quickly to a manageable consistency. This process can be speeded up by placing the mix on a plaster batt or another absorbent surface. Do not allow it to dry out too much. Wedge thoroughly to get rid of any uneven lumps and continue to wedge until the clay feels plastic and smooth but not sticky. It is now ready to use.

Roll out about three-quarters of the black clay and bag the remaining quarter. Cut 20 inset tiles with the square template and leave to dry to soft leather.

INLAYING Starting with the white insets, place the star template on a tile and draw around it with the potter's needle. Cut into the tile $\frac{1}{8}$ in (3 mm) deep with a wire modelling tool, following the inside line of the star as shown on page 69, and level off. Sharpen the edges of the star with the craft knife. Re-wrap and move on to the next inset.

Take a piece of black clay about the size of a walnut and press firmly into a white inset and re-wrap. Do this to all the white tiles. Fill the black insets with white clay and re-wrap. Leave all the insets under wrap for about 24 hours.

Remove the insets one at a time. Use the steel palette to scrape off the excess colored clay until the star is flush with the background, as shown on page 69. If the star has a blurred edge, allow it to dry a little and re-scrape. When all the tiles are cleaned up, true the edges with the surform and sponge the edges smooth, taking care not to smear the faces of the tiles. Allow to dry out very, very slowly, over at least 5 days.

GLAZING AND FIRING When the inset tiles are bone dry, bisque fire the tiles to 2080°F (1140°C). (This is the vitrification temperature of most earthenware clay and will make the tiles impervious to water.) Do not stack the black on white insets in the kiln as the color might bleed.

Remove all the tiles from the kiln. The insets are ready for use but the rectangular field tiles will need to be glazed. Dip them into the cream glaze, allow to dry and wipe the backs and edges with a damp sponge. Glaze fire to 1940–1980°F (1060–1080°C).

The interlocking pattern of this panel
creates an intriguing basketweave effect.
The larger the area you cover with tiles,
the greater the impact will be.

turkish steam room

This design is a complex variation of colors and shapes that I originally designed for a fashionable hotel steam room. The rich alkaline glazes used are known for strength of color and the extraordinary feature of the crackle effect on the surface.

TO PLAN YOUR TILES, PLOT THE FOLLOWING:

For the hexagonal shape, draw a vertical center line $6\frac{1}{4}$ in (160 mm) long. From the base draw a 90 degree point. Measure along each line 3 in (75 mm) and then draw two vertical lines parallel to the center line. Measure $2\frac{1}{2}$ in (60 mm) along both lines, then join to the apex of your center line.

The cream inset tiles are 3 in (75 mm) square. The top triangles have 90 degrees at base, 3 in (75 mm) on each short side. When planning your layout, allow $\frac{1}{8}-\frac{1}{4}$ in (3-5 mm) for each grout line both horizontally and vertically.

skills required
- ☐ rolling out, page 12
- ☐ cutting out, page 14

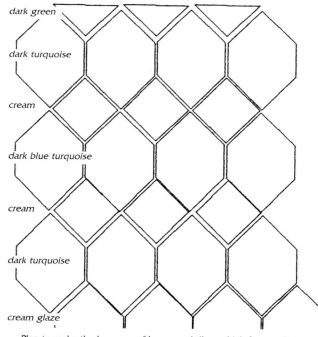

Plan to make the base run of hexagonal tiles, which form a skirting board, half the size of the tiles above.

- ☐ plaster casting and making sprigs, page 17
- ☐ drying out, page 15
- ☐ bisque firing, page 24
- ☐ glazing and firing, page 24

equipment:
batts, buttons for casting, rubber gloves, plaster, rolling pin, guides, calico, fine paintbrush, hexagonal template (see earlier instructions), 2 in (50 mm) square template, 4 x $2\frac{1}{2}$ x $2\frac{1}{2}$ in (100 x 60 x 60 mm) triangular template, craft knife or potter's knife, potter's needle, bowl, water, sponge, plastic scraper or old credit card, steel ruler, toothbrush, surform, paint tray

clay:
To make 30 hexagonal tiles, 10 half-hexagonal tiles, 30 small square tiles and 10 triangular tiles you will need 30 lb (15 kg) white earthenware clay

to make the glaze:
13 oz (375 g) high alkaline frit
3 oz (75 g) china clay
2 oz (50 g) flint
1 pt (500 ml) water

to make the dark turquoise glaze:
Add $\frac{1}{2}$ oz (15g) copper carbonate

to make the dark blue turquoise glaze:
Add 1-3 oz (10 g) copper carbonate and 1-8 oz (2 g) cobalt carbonate

to make the dark green glaze:
Halve the recipe above and add $\frac{1}{4}$ oz (7 g) copper carbonate and $\frac{1}{8}$ oz (2 g) chromium

to make a slightly textured matt cream glaze:
1 pt (500 g) white earthenware glaze
½ oz (15 g) rutile
⅛ oz (3 g) vanadium pentoxide
1 pt (500 ml) water

Make a mould for the sprigged button. Then roll out the clay and leave to dry to soft leather, cut out 35 hexagonal tiles and cut five of these in half to make 10 half hexagons. Using the blunt end of a paintbrush, press a small indentation into the corners as shown below. Leave to dry leather-hard, true the edges and clean with a damp sponge. Allow to dry.

Cut out the 3 in (75 mm) square tiles, leave to dry leather-hard, true and clean up. Allow to dry. Cut out the triangles and leave to dry leather-hard. Using your button mould, press 10 sprigs. Position the sprigs in the centers of the triangles, score with a craft knife and dampen with a tooth-brush. Lay the sprigs in place and press home. True the edges

and clean up, paying attention to the sprigs. Allow to dry. Load the kiln with all tiles and bisque fire to 1830°F (1000°C).

Remove the tiles from the kiln and brush off any dust. Pour the cream glaze into the paint tray, dip in the 3 in (75 mm) tiles and the half hexagon tiles. Wipe the backs and edges clean. Pack them into the kiln on a separate shelf from the rest of the tiles.

Clean out the paint tray and pour in the dark turquoise glaze and dip 15 of the hexagonal tiles. Leave to dry and wipe the backs and edges. Pack into the kiln.

Clean out the tray and pour in the dark blue turquoise glaze, dip the remaining 15 hexagonal tiles. Again leave to dry and clean the backs and edges. Pack into the kiln.

For the last time clean out the tray and add the dark green glaze, dip the sprigged triangular tiles and brush their long edges with glaze. Clean the backs and short edges and pack into the kiln. Glaze fire to 1920–1940°F (1050-1060°C).

Button sprigs add a relief detail to these otherwise simple, glossy tiles.

There are many permutations to the way that these tiles can be laid: you could try introducing a third color
for some of the small squares and disperse them amongst the others to break up the black and white.

jazzy geometric

Based on the simplicity of the clean, crisp lines that are reminisent of Art Deco, this panel uses black and white tiles laid diagonally to form a pattern that carries the eye from bottom to top. The core of the design is focused on three small squares laid vertically point to point, with an L-shaped tile of contrasting color on either side of the center square to form a large square. This is then repeated top and bottom and side to side.

skills required
- ❏ rolling out, page 12
- ❏ cutting out, page 14
- ❏ drying out, page 15
- ❏ mixing and applying glaze, page 22
- ❏ bisque firing, page 24
- ❏ glaze firing, page 24

equipment:
rolling pin, guide, calico, batts, craft knife,
4 x 4 x 2 in (100 x 100 x 50 mm) L-shaped template,
2 in (50 mm) square template,
$\frac{1}{2}$ x 4 in (10 x 100 mm) template,
bowl, water, sponge, paint tray

clay:
To make 40 L-shaped tiles 4 x 4 x 2 in
    (100 x 100 x 50 mm), 2 in (50 mm) square and
    40 border tiles $\frac{1}{2}$ x 4 in (10 x 100 mm) you will need
    15 kg (30 lb) white earthenware clay

to make the glazes:
2 lb (1 kg) shiny white earthenware glaze
2 lb (1 kg) shiny black earthenware glaze

Prepare and roll out the clay and leave to dry to soft leather. Cut out all the tiles, paying particular attention to the corners and the narrow border tiles that are extremely fragile. Leave to dry out to leather-hard, true the edges with the surform and clean up with a damp sponge. Allow the tiles to dry slowly until they are bone dry and then bisque fire them to 1830°F (1000°C).

Take the tiles out of the kiln and remove any dust. Divide the L-shaped and inset tiles into two piles. Pour white glaze into the paint tray, dip half of the L-shaped tiles and insets and set aside to dry. Clean off any glaze from the backs and edges and pack into the kiln. Do not mix the colors in the kiln, use a shelf for the white and another shelf for the black. This will avoid color contamination.

Wash out the paint tray thoroughly and add the black glaze. Dip all the remaining tiles, including the narrow borders, and leave to dry. Clean the backs and edges and pack into the kiln. Glaze fire all the tiles to 1940-1980°F (1060-1080°C).

troubleshooting guide

This is a guide to solving a few of the more basic problems you are likely to encounter. To deal with eventualities not covered here, you will need to refer to a more technical book (see Further Reading page 78).

ROLLING OUT

❑ Slab of clay stretches or breaks easily when handled or sticks to rolling pin.

❑ *The clay is too wet. Leave it to dry out a little.*

❑ The slab has little air bubbles under the surface.

❑ *If there are only one or two, prick them with a potter's needle and smooth with a steel palette. If there are many, it will need to be wedged and rerolled.*

❑ The slab cracks at the edges and is difficult to roll out.

❑ *The clay is too dry. Spray it with water and wrap in polythene to soften.*

CUTTING OUT

❑ The clay sticks to the template or cutter.

❑ *The clay is too wet. Leave it to dry out.*

❑ Clay is difficult to cut out and the edges crumble.

❑ *Clay is too dry. Spray with water and wrap, or try using a sharper knife.*

DIPPING SLIP

❑ The tile is very soft and breaks up.

❑ *Tile is too wet. Abandon it and let the rest of the tiles dry out more.*

❑ Slip cracks on the tile.

❑ *The tile is either too dry or the slip is too thick. If the cracks are very fine, spray with water and wrap to soften, then smooth with a steel palette. If the cracks are large and the slip doesn't break off, either abandon or utilise the texture by coating with a thick coat of glaze later. If the cracks are large and the slip breaks off – abandon!*

BISQUE FIRING

❑ The tile has a chunk blown out from the back.

❑ *There are four possible causes:*
1. The tile was still damp – only fire when the clay is absolutely dry.
2. The firing was too fast at the early stage – reduce the rate of firing for the first four hours.
3. The tiles were stacked too high.
4. Foreign bodies may have contaminated the tiles.

❑ The tiles have small cracks on the edges.

❑ *The tiles were too dry when wiped with a damp sponge. Always clean up the tiles when damp. Alternatively, there was an air bubble (see Rolling Out above).*

GLAZED TILES

❏ The glaze has crawled in odd patches.
❏ *The surface of the bisque was dusty or greasy – ensure tiles are kept clean and covered if not glazed immediately. Try putting a blob of glaze in the crawled place and refire.*

❏ The glaze has crawled in larger areas.
❏ *The glaze was probably applied too thick – abandon the tile!*

❏ Tile feels rough and the glaze is patchy.
❏ *Glaze was applied too thin. Warm the tile to 108°F and reglaze with a thicker coat. Then refire.*

❏ Tiles appear slightly matt when they should have a high gloss.
❏ *The glaze is underfired. Refire 48°F-68°F higher, or if at the bottom of kiln, place at the top in your next firing.*

❏ Tile has lots of small sharp blisters.
❏ *The glaze was fired too high, sometimes refiring 48°F-68°F lower wiil rectify this problem. Do further firings at the lower temperature.*

❏ Larger tiles have cracked or split after firing.
❏ *There are two causes:*
1. The tile was under stress. Lay it on a bed of alumina, or prop it up off the shelf.
2. The kiln was cooled too fast. Leave vent plugs closed and cool naturally away from draughts.

glossary

BISQUE (OR BISCUIT) FIRING
Firing clay to a hard substance.

CLAY MEMORY
Tendency for clay to revert to its original shape.

DIE
A metal disc with a shaped hole which is fitted to a clay gun. The clay is forced through the disc to form long, thin shapes which are used as relief patterns or borders.

EARTHENWARE
A type of fired clay that is still porous.

EXTRUSIONS
Clay that has been forced through a plastic or metal die, creating a continuous strip or moulding.

FRIT
Glaze compounds that have been made safe or practical to use.

GLAZE (OR GLOST) FIRING
Firing to make the glaze form a glassy surface.

SLIP
Mixture of clay and water.

SPRIGGING
Applying a wet relief motif on to a wet surface.

VITRIFICATION
Heating a material until it melts to a glass-like substance. In ceramics, the process is halted before the material loses its shape.

WEDGING
Kneading clay in a ball to produce a homogenous consistency.

further reading

HISTORICAL

Islamic Tiles, Venetia Porter, Interlink Publishing Group, 1995

The Decorative Tile, Tony Herbert and Kathryn Huggins, Phaidon Press, 1995

Moorish Architecture in Andalusia, Marianna Barrucand and Achim Bednorz, Taschen America, 1996

The Best of Pottery, Jonathan Fairbanks and Angela Fina, North Light Books, 1996

TILES

Hand Crafted Ceramic Tiles, Janis Fanning and Mike Jones, Sterling Publications, 1998

Handmade Tiles, Frank Giorgini, Lark Books, 1994

Tile Style Pattern Guide, Jill Blake, Knickerbocker Press, 1996

GENERAL

Potter's Manual, Kenneth Clark, Book Sales, 1991

The Complete Potter's Companion, Tony Birks, Bulfinch Press, 1998

The Potter's Dictionary of Material and Techniques, Frank Hamer and Janet Hamer, University of Pennsylvania Press, 1997

The Illustrated Dictionary of Practical Pottery, Robert L Fournier, Chilton Book Co., 1992

The Potter's Complete Book of Clay and Glazes, James Chappell, Watson-Guptill, 1991

The Big Book of Ceramics: A Guide to the History, Materials, Equipment and Techniques of Hand-Building, Molding, Throwing, Kiln-Firing and Glazing, Joaquim Chavarria, Watson-Guptill, 1994

Handbuilt Ceramics: Pinching, Coiling, Extruding, Molding, Slip Casting, Slab Work, Kathy Triplett, Lark Books, 1997

stockists & suppliers

Aardvark Clay Co.
1400 E. Pomona Street
Santa Ana, CA 92705
Tel: 714-541-4157
Fax: 714-541-2021

Amherst Potters Supply
47 East Street
Hadley, MA 01035
Tel: 413-586-4507
Fax: 413-584-5535

American Art Clay Company, Inc.
4717 W. 16th Street
Indianapolis, IN 46222
Tel: 800-374-1600
Fax: 317-248-9300

Bennett's Pottery Supply
431 Enterprise Street
Ocoee, FL 34761
Tel: 800-432-0074

Ceramic Supply of NY and NJ
7 Route 46, West
Lodi, NJ 07644
Tel: 201-340-3005

Continental Clay Company
1101 Stinson Blvd., NE
Minneapolis, MN 55413
Tel: 800-432-CLAY
Fax: 612-331-8564

Kickwheel Pottery Supply
6477 Peachtree Industrial Blvd.
Atlanta, GA 30360
Tel: 800-241-1895

Leslie Ceramics Supply Co., Inc.
1212 San Pablo Avenue
Berkley, CA 94706
Tel: 510-524-7363
Fax: 510-524-7040

Miami Clay Co.
270 N.E. 183 Street
Miami, FL 33179
Tel: 305-651-4695
Fax: 305-652-8498

Minnesota Clay USA
8001 Grand Avenue South
Bloomington, MN 55420
Tel: 612-884-9101

Seattle Pottery Supply
35 South Hanford
Seattle, WA 98134
Tel: 800-522-1975
Fax: 206-587-0373

index